The Q.U.E.S.T. for Vocation

*A Personal Journey
to Discern
a Life's Calling*

**QUINCY D. BROWN
Foreword by Shirley J. Roels**

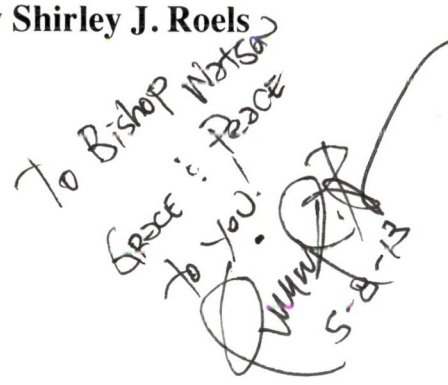

PRAISE FOR
THE Q.U.E.S.T FOR VOCATION

ಬ

"Joseph Campbell showed us the importance of hearing a calling. Now, Quincy Brown gives us an essential handbook to the hidden dimensions of the journey. *The Q.U.E.S.T. for Vocation* reveals the rewarding pilgrimage to a sense of true purpose."

Jonathan Young, Psychologist
Founding Curator, Joseph Campbell Archives

"One of the hallmarks of the heirs of John Wesley, the founder of Methodism, is a plain and straightforward theology. In *The Q.U.E.S.T for Vocation,* Quincy Brown has given us a theology that is both plain and poetic. This book and his life are a fine combination of creativity and stability, of childlike playfulness and mature wisdom."

John Simmons
St. James United Methodist Church

"In form and in practice, Quincy Brown's book *The Q.U.E.S.T. for Vocation* encourages the reader to look beyond the ways he or she has habitually approached life and faith. As readers finish this book, they will recognize their calling to attend to their own Q.U.E.S.T."

Bridgette Young Ross
Assistant General Secretary for Collegiate Ministry

"In *The Q.U.E.S.T. for Vocation*, Quincy Brown provides a way to help us to walk beside others in discerning the calling upon their lives. Perhaps one of the most important things that come from this book is the fact that when we truly accept the call of God, there is no turning back."

Emile Ennis
retired United Methodist minister

"Often we do not pay attention to the things that God really is using to get our attention, instead listening to the 'outer voices' that many times want to keep us at a status quo...or living a life that is not really ours to live if we want to live our soul calling. *The Q.U.E.S.T. for Vocation* is such a treasure chest of images, ideas, places to pay attention, ideas to ponder that really brings the truth to pursuing a life's calling."

Gini Norris-Lane
Schreiner University

"Every person, on and off the campus, who is either assisting persons or who is exploring a call for themselves, must read this book."

Luther Felder
Paine College

The Q.U.ES.T. for Vocation:
A Personal Journey
to Discern a Life's Calling

Quincy D. Brown

xulon
PRESS

Copyright © 2013 by Quincy D. Brown

The Q.U.E.S.T. for Vocation
by Quincy D. Brown

Printed in the United States of America

ISBN 9781626973336

All rights reserved solely by the author. The author guarantees all contents are original and do not infringe upon the legal rights of any other person or work. No part of this book may be reproduced in any form without the permission of the author. The views expressed in this book are not necessarily those of the publisher.

Unless otherwise noted, the Scripture quotations contained herein are from the New Revised Standard Version Bible. Copyright © 1989 by the Division of Christian Education of the National Council of Churches of Christ in the U.S.A. Used by permission. All rights reserved.

All stories are based on encounters with individuals or composites of several persons, but for the sake of anonymity, names and circumstances have been altered.

www.xulonpress.com

To Dionne.
For your inspiration, encouragement,
prayers, love, and care.

Contents
ಬ

Foreword by Shirley J. Roels xi
Acknowledgements. xvii

PART ONE: *The Intellectual Call of the Mind*

1. The Voice Calls 21
2. Listening for a Life's Calling. 34
3. The Call of Order in the Midst of Chaos 50
4. The Call from Childhood Fascinations 60
5. The Call of a New Self-Image 75

PART TWO: *The Physical Call from the Body*

6. The Call to Enter the Unknown 89
7. The Call of the Dark Night of the Soul 99
8. The Call of Suffering and Pain 112
9. The Call of Curing and Healing. 126
10. The Call of Devastating News. 140
11. Missing the Call. 156

Part Three: *The Call of the Soul*

12. The Call of Imagination and Soul 173
13. The Call of the Music Within. 195

Part Four: *The Call to Meaningful Work*

14. The Journey to a Career and Calling 205
15. The Call to Serve the Church. 218

Conclusion 239

Foreword

ಬ

We live in fragmented times when we rarely sense a larger tide of history that sweeps in one clear and prevailing direction. Instead, there's whitewater turbulence, yin and yang, up and down, here and there, all crashing together, frequently in an impersonal cacophony. For all of the freedom that comes with such variety, it also becomes tougher to find our place as well as our voice when a dominant cultural narrative does not prevail. In such a space, we need each other's stories, to provide encouragement on the journey and to remind us that we are not alone.

Each of our stories is intimately intertwined with the stories of close family members, teachers, mentors, heroes, plants, and animals. We are also affected by those we counsel closely, people we see at a distance, and even the writers who shape our fantasies. Such a special confluence of influences makes each of our stories a distinct but not isolated tale. Their development depends on the interchange between our inner selves and experiences with creation as well as the meaning that we teased out of these intersections. Such freedom may feel more like a patchwork quilt. But by exploring our narratives, we create whole cloth from the fabric of our choices.

As a fellow traveler, Quincy Brown contributes to the wholeness each of us seeks through *The Q.U.E.S.T. for Vocation*. Since he is the LaGrange College Vice President for Spiritual Life and Church Relations, one might imagine it as a story of success and triumph, one that highlights a rise into professional influence. While that's true, this tome is also a narrative about life as he is living it and about the mysterious ways of God. Quincy writes as a person who has been humbled and sometimes left without easy answers.

Quincy's confluence of calling is not the one that he would have imagined as a youngster, or likely the one that either of his parents would have envisioned. It is not Quincy's preferred plot, in which a superhero prevails against the odds because of personal strength and a sense of public duty. Quincy's story is not an easy script where might and right win the day. Instead, it is a tale of hope and struggle about identity, health, challenges, and gifts. This is a book that prompts deeper questions about the purpose of existence.

Additionally, this is a story with color as one of its themes. Race, like gender, class, and other sources of social shaping, is one important element in Quincy's narrative.

Foreword

He readily describes how being African-American has affected his life and times, sometimes in surprising and even twisted ways. But the authenticity with which he describes his experience is useful to us all as we consider how our particular backgrounds connect each of us with society in our time. It will help us ponder how we claim our identities without being trapped by particular histories.

So this book is an honest and intimate story about a real life as it unfolds with all its twists and turns. Quincy's reflections explore life as he is living it in ways that have encouraged him to reflect on the meaning of being an individual who is also connected to the ways of God. Quincy's story becomes a path to explore a larger story, in which the life and times of one person are woven with the Creator's intentions for the universe. It is a story of leading the life to which he is continuously called and of *The Voice* who goes behind, before, and with him.

Quincy's reflections weave Scripture, the tradition of a great cloud of witnesses, and reason with his personal experience. He lives his surprising life as a finite human for whom daily living can seem piecemeal, cruel, contradictory, or terribly perplexing. So Quincy turns to Scripture for important reference points to undergird his continuing faith and hope. He believes that Scripture has authority regarding the big questions that he is asking about sickness, health, brokenness, and contribution.

The Q.U.E.S.T. for Vocation

But his reflections extend beyond biblical quotations. He reflects on witnesses to faith and hope from early human times, many of whom are characters in the Old or New Testaments. He comments on those who throughout history—whether philosophers or theologians, the enslaved or the freed, poets or artists—have asked big questions about meaning and sought helpful interpretations of their worthy dreams. These reflections enrich his story and connect it to each of ours.

Finally, Quincy connects reason to experience. While he embraces the mysterious ways of God, he does so while remaining a thinking man. His life experience does not allow him to be swept away by pious platitudes. He seeks reasoned ways to position his life experience in a deeper river of belief, hope, creativity, and joy. His struggles with kidney failure are not, in the end, a sad tale of sound and fury, signifying nothing. Instead, the story that Quincy tells is framed by Biblical faith and reason assisted by the mysterious presence that we often call the Holy Spirit. So Scripture, tradition, reason, and experience all flow together in his writing.

The Q.U.E.S.T. for Vocation illustrates vocation, a sense of living before God's face with life of purpose and determination in the midst of fragmented cacophony and circumstances beyond one's personal control. Quincy's reflections and his questions are a call to faith as described

Foreword

in Hebrews 11:1: "Now faith is the assurance of things hoped for, the conviction of things not seen." It is a commentary in which his personal story is enveloped by the larger story of a God who loves us deeply and continues to walk with us. Reading his words will encourage the exploration of your own questions about faith, hope, and love.

Shirley J. Roels, PhD.
Senior advisor for NetVUE (the Network for Vocation in Undergraduate Education)
The Council of Independent Colleges
January 2013

Acknowledgements
ಐ

Writing a book, like living life, is a quest, and it is best done with the support of community. This book is filled with ideas that are not uniquely my own. A number of people, in both large and small ways, have walked alongside me to contribute to the writing and publication of this book.

Several friends provided the necessary support by offering valuable suggestions as I was writing this book. I am grateful to Laura Faulkner, Luther Felder, Shirley Roels, Jack Slay, Sharon Daloz Parks, Mary Lou Boice, Jonathan Young, B. Michael Watson, Lesley Baskette, John Simmons, Gini Norris-Lane, Emile Ennis, Bridgette Young Ross, George Thompson, Jr., David Garrison, and Leon Matthews, Jr. for their proof-reading and suggestions.

To them, I am deeply indebted and grateful. I also wish to thank the students I worked with over the past sixteen years in my work as chaplain and Vice President for Spiritual Life and Church Relations. Their stories and experiences were invaluable in helping me tie together the pieces for this book.

I extend my heartfelt gratitude to my publisher, Xulon Press, for giving me the opportunity to publish my discoveries from my Q.U.E.S.T.$_{TM}$ to discern a life's calling. A debt of gratitude is owed to Laine Scott for her patience and editorial skills. Her work with the manuscript has, in every case, enabled me to say more clearly and with greater precision what I intended to say. I am grateful for our collaboration.

Part One

The Intellectual Call of the Mind

CHAPTER ONE

The Voice Calls

ಙ

For as long as I can remember, I have been preoccupied with questions about vocation. What does it mean to find and follow a personal calling? How do we know what we are meant to do with our precious time and talents and treasure during our short lives here on earth? How, exactly, do we "hear" calls anyway? What happens if we miss our calling—maybe because we fail to hear it or don't have the courage to follow it?

—John Neafsey[1]

When they came, he looked on Eliab and thought, "Surely the Lord's anointed is now before the Lord." But the Lord said to Samuel, "Do not look on his appearance or on the height of his stature, because I have rejected him; for the Lord does not see as mortals see; they look on the outward appearance, but the Lord looks on the heart."
—1 Samuel 16:6-7

Everyone needs a reason to get up in the morning. Whether it is for our families, our jobs, or contributing to the larger society, we all have a natural reason for being. When we listen to and follow our *life's calling*, it gives us a sense of purpose.

From birth to death, we are on a quest to discover this calling. But listening to a life's calling is not always easy. The call can literally catch us off-guard and require us to act in ways that seem contradictory and strange to our friends and family. These calls can sometimes come at the strangest of times, as Ray Kinsella discovers.

In the film *Field of Dreams*, novice farmer Ray Kinsella is caught off-guard while walking in his cornfield. A *voice* calls him to follow a dream that will change his life.[2] The voice calls to him, saying, "If you build it, he will come," and Ray sees a baseball diamond in the cornfield. Ray's wife, Annie, is skeptical, but she allows him to plow under his corn to build the field.

In a similar way, thousands of years earlier, in the Fertile Crescent of the Middle East, the life of the future patriarch Abraham is interrupted by a voice that also appears out of nowhere, calling him to:

> Go from your country and your kindred and your father's house to the land that I will show you. I will make of you a great nation, and I will bless you and make your name great, so that you will be a blessing. I will bless those who bless you, and the one who curses you I will curse; and in you all the families of the earth shall be blessed.[3]

The Voice Calls

Following the Voice

Both Ray and Abraham are introduced to the *voice* who abruptly calls them to leave what is comfortable and familiar, and both embark on a quest towards an adventure of faith. For Ray, this means enduring the skepticism of his wife, Annie, and facing possible financial ruin. Ray and Annie discuss replanting the corn, but because their daughter, Karin, is moved by a vision of Shoeless Joe Jackson, a dead baseball player idolized by Ray's father, and the other seven Chicago Black Sox players (who were banned from baseball for throwing the 1919 World Series) playing in the field of dreams, they decide to listen to the voice. For Abraham, this also means struggling with skepticism as he continues to ask the voice to confirm the initial call to leave his comfort zone, the promise to be the Father of many nations and to live in the Promised Land.

Though unknown to them both, answering the voice (the call) will alter their lives by inviting them to develop a new level of trust and faith. Ray is unaware that answering the voice by building a baseball field in a rural Iowa corn field will open a metaphysical door to his past and to his future. Abraham has no idea that the voice's plan is to shape a clan of people out of a childless marriage by leading them to a new land that the voice promises one day would be their own. This plan will become Abraham's new life's calling: the faithful one who receives the call to move from nomadic living to settle and live in relationship with neighbors in surrounding lands. By answering the call, Abraham becomes the patriarch in Jewish, Muslim, and Christian traditions.

When we are called by the voice, it changes our lives and starts us on a life journey that we never imagined. At the heart of every life's calling is the voice that tells us that we have to change the way we do things. It is the voice that tells us that this person or that person is going to be important in our lives, the voice that tells us that the time has come to move in another direction. It constantly calls to us, asking us to consider who we really are at the core of our being, what we want to accomplish in life, and how we should go about accomplishing that which will ultimately change us to change the world around us.

The Q.U.E.S.T.

Like Ray and Abraham, I have received earth-shattering news from an abrupt *voice* calling me to change my life's plans and direction. In 2008, I wrote my first book about that major change. The book is titled *Q.U.E.S.T: Stories as Guides Through Life's Transitions*,[4] and it examines my need to Question, Uncover, Experience, Search, and Transform (Q.U.E.S.T.$_{TM}$[5]) my life's story during my health struggles of dealing with kidney disease, dialysis, kidney transplantation, and kidney rejection. By using the lens of my own personal experiences, stories from the Bible, and popular culture to help to make sense of things, the book focuses on providing a framework to help individuals walk through the transitional moments of life. After coming through the difficult health crisis with a new understanding of myself and God's grace and care, I discovered that Q.U.E.S.T.$_{TM}$ is actually a discernment process that has helped me to answer a life's calling.

The Q.U.E.S.T.$_{TM}$ process places emphasis on reflecting on my life's experiences to discover my core story and its relation to God's story (Question). After I discovered my story, I began reflecting on the plots and repetitive themes (Uncover). Next, I had to learn to uncover my fundamental assumptions about the world, faith, and God, and to name my feelings and confront the unconscious emotions that affected my behavior (Experience). After these three stages, I was able to sort through my story and find meaning in it by comparing it to other stories (Search). With new meaning assigned to my life's story, I became capable of creating a new story to live by that includes themes from biblical stories (Transform).

Now, five years later, my Q.U.E.S.T.$_{TM}$ to answer a life's calling has led to the writing of this book. Writing this book has served as a way for me to express and pull together insights about vocational discernment from both my personal spiritual journey and my professional life as a minister.

For some time now, I have had a hunch that an important part of my own calling is to help other people to discover their calling. A second kidney transplant from an unknown donor helped to clarify this hunch and served as a harbinger to begin the process of following a Q.U.E.S.T.$_{TM}$ for vocation. I was humbled to know that because someone had died, I now had another chance at life. This knowledge has had a profound effect on me and has prompted me to share my experiences.

The Q.U.E.S.T. for Vocation is the result of the call to make sense of my life's journey to become a whole[6] person: integrating mind, body, and soul in order to engage in meaningful work. Throughout *The Q.U.E.S.T. for Vocation*, I will revisit some of my health experiences with an eye towards how these experiences have helped me to answer a life's calling.

A fundamental assumption behind this book, which is similar to any Q.U.E.S.T.$_{TM}$ for a life's calling, is the deep yearning for a connection with God. It is a quest for making peace with God, known as "at-one-ment" with God's call to search for broader meaning for our lives so that we may do more than we think possible. This at-one-ment involves the continual journey to be undivided within myself and to be "at one" (peace) with God through dying to self-centeredness.

The prevailing approach of this work is the telling of stories, including biographical, autobiographical, and fictional narratives from literature, comic books, and film, to help discern a calling. A life's calling is always a personal story amidst other stories, as all of these stories unfold within the story of God. Some may object to my blending of fictional narratives with biblical stories to discern a life's calling, but some of the great Christian thinkers, such as C.S. Lewis and G.K. Chesterton, found great truths in fictional narratives. For instance, in Chesterton's chapter titled "The Ethics of Elfland" from his book *Orthodoxy*, he sets out to prove there is much to learn from child's fairy tales.[7] Similarly, Lewis combines myth and legends in his great series *The Chronicles of Narnia* to teach his readers about the Christian faith.[8]

I am a right-brained thinker.[9] This means I am more of a creative thinker who uses feeling, intuition, and holy hunches[10] to gather information. Left-brained thinking is just the opposite and focuses on gathering information through logical thinking, analysis, and accuracy. As a right-brained thinker, I tend to retain information through the use of images and patterns by visualizing the "whole" picture first and then working backwards to put the pieces together to create the "whole" picture. Much of my life's

Q.U.E.S.T.[TM] focuses on accepting my natural bent of being a right-brained thinker and learning to integrate left-brained thinking without placing one mode of thinking over the other.

Because of my penchant for right-brained thinking, I am also influenced by a Jungian[11] viewpoint—the inclusion of symbols, epic stories, nightly dreams, metaphors, and images to help us discern messages from our souls—which I use as a lens to view a life's calling to address the emotional, spiritual, and psychological suffering that disconnects us from God and our innermost core that guides the development of our unique selves.

Coupled with this viewpoint is another assumption grounded in the Christian tradition, especially its emphasis on and embrace of narrative. This includes a distinguished lineage incorporating the many stories of the Bible, the work of Church fathers and mothers (including St. Augustine's *Confessions*, 17th-century self-examining Puritan autobiographies, and the 18th-century conversion narratives of Anglican preachers/priests and founders of Methodism, Charles and John Wesley), and the evangelical practice of publically sharing a personal testimony, to tell stories that connect personal stories to God's story and our life's calling.

This book is divided into four sections to highlight several types of callings. Each section provides insight into how a life's calling influences the whole of our lives. Many

The Voice Calls

of the reflections and stories about vocation will present both spiritual and psychological perspectives. Some people will be more familiar and comfortable with using spiritual language in general and the Christian language in particular when it comes to describing their sense of vocation, while others may explain their callings in secular or psychological terms.

Ultimately, however, the language that we choose to use when discussing vocation is less important than the sincerity, thoughtfulness, and openness of the process of self-examination and reflection. The primary ways to use this book are to

- *listen deeply and carefully for the unique and personal ways that the voice of vocation may be expressing itself in your life;*
- *engage in a thoughtful process of discernment and reflection on the unfolding process of your calling; and,*
- *make intelligent and courageous choices to follow where the voice of vocation seems to be leading or calling.*

A Note about Calling and Vocation

I use the words "calling" and "vocation" interchangeably to help us determine our sense of calling that is not a once-and-for-all event. There are several callings that we will receive through our lives, and making "callings" plural gives us the sense that we are in the call-and-response process all the time.

Many of the discussions focus on "personal callings" and "calling with a capital C," which is concerned with the total, permanent, formal, irrevocable giving of self to God in religious service. Listening to either type of calling involves asking thought-provoking questions about our life experiences and the willingness to listen to the *voice*—the still, small voice of God that empowers us to take action, learn, grow, and ultimately become more of whom God has called us to become.

The stories and research insights throughout these pages are meant to inspire and give practical knowledge that we can apply to our calling and vocation. The discernment questions at the end of each chapter are meant to give clarity about what steps to take next. Many of the questions derive from three fundamental questions when discerning a life's calling:

"What has my life been trying to do with me?"

"What has my life been preparing me for?" and

"Who is my life calling me to become?"

Do not skip over these questions. Resist the urge to hurry through this process. Instead, savor it. If taken seriously and patiently, the questions will begin to spur the voice within to help you experience real change and growth before finishing this book.

The Voice Calls

As a minister who engages in pastoral counseling with others, I know that there is usually some conscious or unconscious call that brings us to any destination where we find ourselves. Each of us can look back on our lives to see the direction of that call. Perhaps this look back will cause you to wonder about the calling in your life—its meaning, direction, and purpose.

The Q.U.E.S.T. for Vocation is an invitation to you to turn your attention to the voice that calls to you. I invite you to reflect on your life story as a response to a calling. In exploring the summons that call us into a season of discernment, the book highlights several formative experiences and stories from former college students whom I have counseled in my role as their college chaplain. Throughout these pages you will enter into the process of listening to your life in search of your own vocation. It is in this spirit that I offer what I have learned in the hope that this book might resonate with you during your Q.U.E.S.T.$_{TM}$ for a life's calling.

Questions
1. Have you ever experienced a calling from the voice or sensed a time where your life would no longer be the same?

2. How did you respond to the voice's call?

3. Reflect on the following questions: What has my life been trying to do with me? What has my life been preparing me for? and Who is my life calling me to be?

Notes

1. John Neafsey. *A Sacred Voice Is Calling: Personal Vocation and Social Conscience*. (Mary Knoll: Orbis Books, 2006).

2. *Field of Dreams*. Dir. Phil Robinson. Perf. Kevin Costner, James Earl Jones, Amy Madigan, Burt Lancaster and Ray Liotta. Universal Pictures, 1989. Film.

3. Genesis 12:1-3.

4. Quincy D. Brown. *Q.U.E.S.T.: Stories as Guides Through Life's Transitions*. (Boyd Publishing Company: Milledgeville, GA, 2008).

5. As the name implies, in a quest the main character is looking for something that he expects to find, or he is following some sort of urge that will significantly change his life. The problem is that in the Q.U.E.S.T.$_{TM}$ or vocation, the answers are not forthcoming; it requires us to place our trust and faith in a Presence that is much larger than ourselves.

6. I use the word "whole," which is synonymous with the New Testament Greek word *sozo*. Professor Dwight Judy, Professor Emeritus of Spiritual Formation at Garrett-Evangelical Theological Seminary, suggests that *sozo* is also the same word as "salvation." Wholeness, then, is God's work of offering us healing, balance, and harmony of body, mind, spirit, and relationships through confession, forgiveness, and reconciliation.

Dwight H. Judy. *Discerning Life Transitions: Listening Together in Spiritual Direction.* (New York: Morehouse Publishing, 2010).

7. G.K. Chesterton. *Orthodoxy.* (United Kingdom: Popular Classics Publishing, 2012).

8. C.S. Lewis. *The Chronicles of Narnia.* (New York: HarperCollins Children's Books, 1954).

9. Based on the lateralization of brain function, the right brain-left brain theory grew out of the work of Roger W. Sperry, who was awarded the Nobel Prize in 1981. While studying the effects of epilepsy, Sperry discovered that cutting the corpus collosum (the structure that connects the two hemispheres of the brain) could reduce or eliminate seizures.

10. According to Bruce Main, a "holy hunch" is the phenomenon that takes place when we feel compelled to move in a God-inspired direction. He suggests that perhaps theologically heavy words, such as "calling" and "vocation," need to move aside and give room to more earthy words, such as "hunch" or "nudge." Hunches come to those who take the time to open themselves to the Spirit of God and prompt us to put our faith into action. Bruce Main. *Holy Hunches: Responding to the Promptings of God.* (Grand Rapids: Baker Books, 2007).

11. A Jungian viewpoint comes from Carl Jung's depth psychology. Jung believed that each of us has a specific nature and a calling that is unique to us.

Chapter Two

Listening for a Life's Calling
ಌ

To listen seems like such an ordinary thing; perhaps we too readily underestimate its extraordinary value;... the essential role it can play deserves a closer examination. What might it mean if the people of God had open ears? We need to open our own ears to hear what it means to listen for the soul, and in particular, to discover how we might become habitual in practicing such listening.

—Jean Stairs[1]

We know that all things work together for good for those who love God, who are called according to his purpose.
—Romans 8:28

When the subject of a life's calling comes up, two of the first questions people ask are "How do I know what God is calling me to do?" and "If God is calling me to do or be something special with my life, am I capable or even willing to be or do what or who God requests of me?" This was my case, and if you are reading this book, then there is a strong chance that this is also the case for you.

My sense is that most of us have to thoroughly review the plots of our life's story and experiences in order to see the thread that pulls the tapestry of our lives together into a meaningful pattern. When following a life's calling, our fundamental assumptions of how life operates will be challenged. Just as the Old Testament prophet Ezekiel's call[2] in Babylon challenged the existing assumption that God was limited to only the Temple in Jerusalem, often a life's calling will cause us to reexamine the things that we have accepted to be true.

Catholic philosopher and writer Antonin Sertillanges[3] claims that the intellectual call of the mind is a calling to discover, articulate, and transmit *truth*. Sertillanges sees the intellectual life as essentially a *vocation*. And, in the most spiritual sense of the word, it is, as he says, "a sacred call." Seen through this lens, discerning a vocation is an obligation for every human being to develop his or her intellectual life, since the intellect is at the heart of our being, and our job in life is, if nothing else, the care of the soul.

Our life's calling will abruptly cause us to examine our fundamental assumptions, to question our value system, and to change our future behavior. This review requires carefully listening for God's call in our lives, which is often muffled by the sounds and sights of what seems to be more adventuresome and rewarding, as a young stonecutter discovers.

The Q.U.E.S.T. for Vocation

The Stonecutter

Once upon a time there lived a young boy who wanted to be a stonecutter. He worked for twelve years learning to cut large granite boulders from the bottom of the mountain near his village. One day, as he was cutting through the rock, a merchant happened by. The boy was awestruck by all of the items that the man had for sale.

"I wish I were a merchant," said the boy, and amazingly, his wish was granted. As the boy began selling the merchandise, he heard a small voice advising him to return to his labors as a stonecutter. He ignored this strange voice.

After acquiring many riches, the boy saw a parade pass his little shop. Spying a prince dressed in untold splendor, he said to himself, "I wish I were a prince," and he became one. But as soon as he had become a prince, the same strange voice whispered, "Go back to being a stonecutter." He ignored the voice.

The next day, he stepped outside in his royal apparel and felt the hot sun beating cruelly upon his golden crown. "Even a prince cannot stay cool in the sun," he thought to himself. While wiping the sweat from his brow with a silk handkerchief, he then thought, "It would be nice to be the sun." Immediately his wish was granted, but that same annoying voice told him, "Being the sun is not such a bright idea. Go back to being a stonecutter." Again, he ignored its advice.

Listening for a Life's Calling

The next day while soaring across the morning sky, an unexpected cloud came between the boy and the earth. "That cloud overshadows me," he said to himself. "I wish I were a cloud." Again his wish was granted, but the voice returned saying, "There's a silver lining in every dark cloud. Go back to being a stonecutter."

Turning his thoughts away from the voice, the boy came to a mountain. Despite his best effort, he could not rise above the tall peak. "This mountain is greater than I," he said. "I wish I were a mountain." He became a mountain. Once more the voice from within came to him saying, "Ain't no mountain high enough. Please go back to being a stonecutter." Once more, the boy ignored the voice.

Time went on and the boy-mountain grew older. One day, another stonecutter climbed the young man's side and began chipping away at the rock. Surprised by the pain of the pickaxe digging into his side, the man-mountain yelled, "Ouch! Oooohhhh! Someone is burrowing into my side!" And looking down, he saw that it was a stonecutter that he himself had once been. He said to himself, "That young man is more powerful than I. I wish I were a stonecutter!"

The circle was completed, and the voice said to him, "You have found your calling. You have listened to your inner voice and discovered your true identity!"

What is a Calling?

The stonecutter's story, adapted from a Chinese fable[4], illustrates the importance of listening to a calling. Throughout life, a calling surfaces over and over again, sometimes in obscure ways or in areas that we have ignored. It could be said that everyone has a calling and that all of us—whether or not we are aware of it or respond to it—have the potential to hear and follow a unique and personal calling in our own lives.

Often we are "called," "nudged," or "prompted" by a powerful inner knowing and unshakable conviction that this or that is the right thing to do. Simply put, we must honor that which we are called to be.

Our calling can also come to us in the most subtle ways—so subtle, in fact, that we often miss what we are being shown. The stonecutter makes the mistake of trying to tell his life what he wants to do with it instead of listening to the voice. For the stonecutter, this means being a merchant, a prince, the sun, and so on. In each of his experiences of trying on another identity, the voice summons him to listen to what his life is telling him: to follow his true calling as a stonecutter.

Listening to Our Lives

Listening to the voice requires some sacrifice for the stonecutter, as he is never quite content with all of the different "identity roles" that do not fit him properly or bring him meaning. His experiences seem to follow a fundamental law of listening to a life's calling: If we have had a sense of our calling, and we do not answer and follow, if we decide to stay where we are because it is safe and secure, then our lives simply dry up and become void of meaning. And like the stonecutter, most of us are likely to hear the voice call to us several times before we realize that we are being called.

When we are finally able to listen to what our lives are calling us to be, we must have ears to hear the difficult truths, experience the tough feelings of doubt and uncertainty, and have the courage to stay with the difficult struggles until resolution. When we are summoned by a calling, we are invited to connect the stories of our lives together in a meaningful way. This includes seeing the connection between our external lives filled with visible plots, facts, and behavior and the internal stories of meaning, emotions, feelings, assumptions, and fears that often go unnoticed. This connection between external and internal stories together to see God's larger story of meaning will be the focus of many of the call experiences that are highlighted throughout the book.

Pastor and author Joanne Blum[5] says that our calling is who we are, and it insists upon being recognized. Saying "yes" to a calling often causes opposing energies to emerge within us, where one part of us thinks that our action is silly and senseless, and the other, which often carries a deep wisdom, knows that our lives will not make sense unless we answer the call.

Gregg Levoy, the bestselling author of *Callings: Finding and Following an Authentic Life*[6], says that the purpose of a call is to summon us away from our daily grinds to a new level of awareness, into a sacred frame of mind that offers communion with that which is bigger than ourselves.

Callings, much like the still small voice that the biblical prophets heard, are filtered through symbols, nightly dreams, happenstances, intuitive hunches, and bodily symptoms. Many of the examples of callings throughout *The Q.U.E.S.T. for Vocation* focus on such experiences.

To Christian believers, a calling is the voice of *vocation* or God's voice speaking in the stirrings of our heart, through meaningful encounters with significant people, or in life experiences that seem to convey an important personal message to us about the direction of our life.

The Call of Vocation

The word *vocation* comes from the Latin, meaning "to be called," and it is rooted in the Latin for "voice." The original meaning of the word *vocation* means "the voice within." There is an importance of the original sense of *vocation* and *calling*, and this "calling" has been known by a variety of names over the centuries.

The ancient Greeks often referred to a person's calling as one's *daimon*, or "guardian spirit," while the Romans would later call it the *genii*, or "genius," meaning "to generate, to beget," implying the voice of the generative process in the individual. Quakers see it as the inner light. Humanist traditions speak of living with integrity or authenticity. Theologian Thomas Merton sees it as a hidden wholeness. From a psychological perspective, vocation originates in our deepest and most authentic self; English pediatrician and psychoanalyst Donald W. Winnicott calls this our "true self."

However we understand it, the sense of vocation is an experience of *someone* or *something* that speaks to our hearts in a compelling way and that calls for us to *listen* and *follow*. This requires, first of all, a capacity to hear the voice as it speaks to us through our life experiences. Once we have heard the call, we then face the challenge of making intelligent, discerning, and courageous choices to follow where it is leading. It is as American poet E.E. Cummings once said: "It takes courage to grow up and become who you really are."

The earliest meanings of the word *vocation* have to do with the experience of being addressed by a voice. But who, or what, is actually doing the calling? How can we understand the voice? Scholars such as Frederick Buechner, Joseph Campbell, Parker Palmer and others have all understood *vocation* as an inner voice that calls each person to his or her unique destiny.

My reading of these scholars suggests that vocation is God's voice calling out to the stirrings of our heart, in our deepest desires, through meaningful encounters with people, or in experiences that seem to convey a message about our ultimate purpose and destiny. The divine source of wisdom, mysteriously both beyond and within ourselves, guides the path of our true calling and summons us to be who we were created to become. The Quaker writer Thomas Kelly puts it this way:

> Deep within us all, there is an amazing inner sanctuary of the soul, a holy place, a Divine Center, a speaking Voice, to which we may continuously return. Eternity is at our hearts, pressing upon our time-torn lives, warming us with imitations of an astounding destiny, calling us home unto itself.[7]

It is important to note that a sense of vocation begins not in what the world needs, but rather in the nature of soul—the human self. In the Old Testament, "soul" is translated from the Hebrew word *nephesh*. In the New Testament, "soul" is translated from the Greek word *psychē*. The words *nephesh* and *psychē* can also be translated as "life" or "self," since both words refer to the totality of the person as a center of life, emotions, feelings, and longings that can be fully realized only in union with God. Based on this, a "calling," or a vocation, is a strong "soulful" impulse inside ourselves that moves us toward a blending of who we really are with what we choose to do—a joining together of self and service.

A true calling recognizes our God-given personal gifts, interests, and personality and finds ways to put them to good use. A vocation can be seen as a calling to actualize or realize our potential in the real world. Vocation grows out of knowing and following the leadings of our own "heart's desire."

Our heart's desire can be seen as God's desire in us, for us, or from us, where the key questions are "What am I good at?" or "What is my gift?" Answering such questions requires a realistic appraisal of the things we do well and the things that we do not do so well.

Sometimes feedback from others (e.g., affirmation of our gifts from a respected mentor) can help us to recognize our strengths and weaknesses in various areas. We can also learn from experiences of failure that teach us painful lessons about what we are not good at. Sometimes a willingness to experiment and "test" our dream in the real world is helpful in the process of discerning whether or not it is realistic or possible for us to achieve or fulfill.

Vocation is ultimately about giving our lives in service for others—giving ourselves away. It entails a Q.U.E.S.T.$_{TM}$ to discern the meaning of our life's journey where many paths will diverge. In addition to service for others, vocation is also about listening to ourselves—listening to the yearning of our souls.

Most of us have never listened to what our lives are saying—we hear only what we are telling our lives to do. This means that we have been absorbing all the words and thoughts and directives of others and have been cramming them into our heads, trying to understand the world and ourselves in it, instead of actively listening to our own lives, the promptings of our souls. Such an endeavor as listening to our lives at the soul level requires courage, systematic reflection, and discipline.

Church History and Vocation

We are called to be the person God created us to be, first, by following Christ and living faithfully. But there is much more to God's call than being a Christian. God calls us to specific actions that reflect our unique gifts, talents, passions, and abilities. This secondary calling is distinct for everyone and moves us to invest our lives in an area of work or community that gives meaning and purpose.

Interpreting vocation broadly and richly from this perspective means discerning a calling or a summons to meaningful living. To receive a call means that someone outside myself is calling; what I am to do in response to that call provides me with purpose; and this call and response occur within and are guided by my larger community.

For many people, however, vocation originates in the church and hints at God calling us to do some type of ministry. For instance, in medieval Europe, practices such as entering the priesthood or joining a religious order were deemed "vocations," or holy callings from God. Later, the early church reformers—Martin Luther, founder of the Lutheran Church, and John Calvin, founder of the Reformed Church—expanded the notion of *vocation* from the Catholic Church's understanding of being called to the priesthood.

Luther held that all Christians share a common "vocation" to love and serve others, and that they carry it out through a variety of specific "vocations" that can range from being a missionary, to milking cows, to teaching grammar to recalcitrant college students. Although some Roman Catholics continue to understand vocation as referring solely to a calling to the priesthood or a religious order, the Second Vatican Ecumenical Council endorsed a wider sense of vocation to include lay people participating in the creative work of God through a variety of efforts.

God Speaks to Us

I believe that God has plans[8] for our lives. Yes, I said *plans*, and not a single plan. For most of us, however, this is a difficult belief to grasp since there are times when we receive messages and clues that point us in the direction that we are born to take, but it does not exactly feel as if God is giving them to us. We may or may not have something inscribed in stone, a burning bush, or something written in the clouds to get our attention.

The Bible contains many reports of a call from God—that at the time seemed contrary to God's calling—to individuals and many different responses to that call. One example is the story of Hannah, a woman who wants to have children but is unable to conceive. Hannah seeks the Lord, asking Him to give her a child and promising that she will give the child back to God as a servant if she is able to conceive.

God hears her prayer, and she gives birth to Samuel, one of the most important leaders in the Old Testament. As she has promised, when he is nearly two years old she gives Samuel back to God by taking the toddler to live at the tabernacle of God.

One night as young Samuel is drifting off to sleep, he hears a voice. Thinking that Eli, the high priest of the tabernacle, is calling to him, he runs to find out what he wants. Eli says that it has nothing to do with him and tells Samuel

Listening for a Life's Calling

to go back to sleep. Any parent who has been awakened in the night can guess the tone of voice that Eli uses!

This happens a second time, with the same result. But when it happens the third time in the same night, Eli finally gets the message. "This is God wanting to speak to you," Eli tells Samuel and then counsels, "Go and lie down, and if He calls you, say, 'Speak, Lord, for your servant is listening.'"[9] Samuel learns from his call that night that a life's calling describes the core purpose of our lives at a given time. Through his early confusing moments of childhood, Samuel follows God's calling that will lead him to become Israel's first major prophet. In the next chapter, we will investigate how following a calling, which leads us into the unknown and unpredictable, challenges our fundamental assumptions about ourselves, God, and the world.

Questions
1. The Stonecutter ignores his innate gifts and talents by chasing the dreams of others, only to have the voice remind him of his life's calling. What are your gifts and talents? Have you ever ignored your calling in exchange for something that you believed was more alluring?

2. Consider how your life has been laced with meaning (if that meaning has had the chance to emerge). Have there been places in your life where you needed to make a choice that could lead you to a greater sense of meaning and purpose?

The Q.U.E.S.T. for Vocation

3. One of Shakespeare's famous lines in *Hamlet*—"This above all, to thine own self be true"—speaks to living an authentic life by following a set of core values of what is truly important to us. Are there ways in which you are not being true to yourself? Are you truly doing what you believe in and living an authentic life?

Notes

1. Jean Stairs. *Listening for the* Soul: Pastoral Care and Spiritual Direction. (Minneapolis: Augsburg Press, 2000), 15.

2. Ezekiel received his prophetic call in the fifth year of the Babylonian Exile during the seventh century BC. The people who were exiled to Babylon thought that all was lost when they were removed from Jerusalem, where God was believed to dwell. For centuries, the prevailing view held by many in Jerusalem was that the Temple stood as the center of the faith of Israel. When the Temple was destroyed and the people had been removed to a strange land, a new notion emerged. The Hebrews discovered that God was not only in Jerusalem, but also even in Babylon. Out of Babylon the Hebrews came away with a new understanding that God was not centered in a geographic place, but rather that God could be found anywhere. Ezekiel and his contemporaries, Isaiah and Jeremiah, discover this also.

3. A.G. Sertillanges. Translated by Mary Ryan. The Intellectual Life: Its Spirit, Conditions, Methods, (Cork: Catholic University of America Press, 1987).

4. "The Stonecutter" is a Chinese folk-tale of unknown authorship. It was first translated by David Brauns in

Japanische Märchen und Sagen in 1885. Andrew Lang drew upon this source to publish his translation of the tale in The Crimson Fairy Book in 1903. Various adaptations of the fable appear across cultures and continents, including "The Fisherman and His Wife" by the Brothers Grimm.

5. Joanne Blum. Living Your Calling. (Lincoln: Writers Club Press, 1999). 5.

6. Gregg Levoy. Callings: Finding and Following an Authentic Life. (Harmony Books: New York, 1997). 2.

7. Thomas R. Kelly. A Testament of Devotion. (San Francisco: HarperCollins Publishers, Inc., 1992).

8. My reading of Jeremiah 29:11 (For surely I know the plans I have for you, says the Lord, plans for your welfare and not for harm, to give you a future with hope) suggests that God's plans are plural and not singular, as popular opinion states. This means that there is a Plan A, B, C, D, and so on. The plan adapts when we partner in relationship with God. This suggests that human will is part of the process and that we can refuse God's calling and plans for our lives, but God does not give up on us so easily.

9. 1 Samuel 3:9.

Chapter Three

The Call of Order in the Midst of Chaos
☙

*There are all different kinds of voices calling you,...
and the problem is to find out which is the voice of God
rather than of society, or the superego, or self-interest.*
—Frederick Buechner[1]

*Very truly, I tell you, unless a grain of wheat falls into
the earth and dies, it remains just a single grain; but if
it dies, it bears much fruit.*
—John 12:24

Elizabeth was a twenty-two-year-old college senior that I worked with a few years ago. She was struggling to discern her life's purpose and direction. Elizabeth was disillusioned with organized religion. She had experienced several interruptions in her life, involving lost relationships that had left her emotionally numb, rebellious, and uncertain.

During a meeting with Elizabeth to work through the pain of her loss, she expressed her contempt for uninspiring

The Call of Order in the Midst of Chaos

church beliefs such as "hell." Her negative experiences of church, as well as the deaths of members of her family, culminated in a wounding of her soul, which ultimately led to a search for new images and to outright rebellion.

She painfully connected the notion of going to hell to being punished for not doing everything she was supposed to do. She blamed her current worldview, best described as a "sort of an agnostic view with remnants of Christianity[2]," for being skeptical of religion but paradoxically prompting her to pray over meals and, periodically, about her struggles.

Elizabeth suggested that her experiences of church during her youth were close to worshipping what she called the "god of orthodoxy," where she was told that unless she followed the "right way," she was doomed and would never be right. As Elizabeth suggests,

> A call or summons from this "false god" is a call that I will not answer. Besides, putting God in a box is not the way it was meant to be. Right now, I'm not practicing any sort of religion, as school has me extremely busy. I do pray about things every once in a while, but the whole religious thing is kind of out there right now. I do believe that there is a God. I just have not found the strength to return to church or decided what I want or need right now.

Typical of many students struggling with trying to make sense of life and college, Elizabeth is what academic scholars

Robert Nash and Michele Murray, in their work with helping college students find purpose, call a "wounded believer."[3]

A wounded believer is a student who defines her or his religious experience as a reaction to the mental and emotional abuse suffered, often perpetuated, in the *name* of religion.

When the Elizabeths of the world suffer from family losses and do not have a safe space to engage in the discernment process to sort things through, it becomes very easy to shut down from hearing a call of any sort. And, like Elizabeth, by the time most college students hit their senior year, they come face-to-face with overwhelming change and the need to sort out new directions for life.

Beginning a new life for students like Elizabeth is comparable to diving into the deep end of the pool. It is exciting and frightening at the same. In my role as college chaplain, I have worked among many young adults who were in the midst of emotional waters. On some days, excitement prevailed; on other days, fear and anxiety were overwhelming. Most of the time, however, students experienced a swirling mixture of all these emotions that felt more like the chaos of being lost in an unexplored wilderness rather than like a dive into a pool.

The Chaotic Wilderness Experience

Elizabeth's story of struggling to make sense of life is common for both young adults and adults alike. As she discovered, it takes courage, patience, and a safe space to begin the Q.U.E.S.T.$_{TM}$ to find meaning and discern a life's calling. Over the last few years, while helping students such as Elizabeth struggle with their own sense of a life calling, I have discovered the importance of this discernment process that brings order out of chaos.

Throughout human history, *chaos* has always been a common term for "the unknown and unpredictable." The fear of chaos is one of the major stumbling blocks to answering a calling, since following an unknown voice or an intuitive hunch without physical evidence often feels more chaotic than benevolent.

In trying to help Elizabeth make sense out of things, I felt as if we were swimming upstream in chaotic waters of episodic nonsense. I suggested that Elizabeth apply the *wilderness*[4] metaphor from the Exodus story to explain what she was experiencing in her struggle. While she was receptive to the idea, she ultimately chose not to pursue this, as she claimed that the experience took too much time away from her studies.

In the Old Testament, the term *wilderness* is also connected with the Hebrew word that is translated as "chaos" from the Genesis creation story. The creation story states that "the earth was a formless void, and darkness covered the face of the deep, while a wind from God swept over the face of the waters."[5] The "formless void" where "darkness covered...the deep" serves as a metaphor to aptly describe times when we experience something unexpected and disappointing or encounter questions that challenge the way we make sense of things.

The wilderness can take many forms, including a family crisis, loss of relationship or identity, a health crisis, the defeat of a cause, betrayal by a community, or intellectual inquiry that poses a challenge to an assumed faith or belief. Our world begins to change and perhaps even falls apart. And yet, as with every wilderness experience, there is also the possibility of eventually finding the "Promised Land."

The wilderness is a difficult place to navigate. In the course of their wilderness wanderings, however, the Israelites found certain markers that served as beacons to guide and sustain them. They were called to follow God through the wilderness by several events, including a cloud by day and a pillar of fire by night, water springing from a rock, and bread falling from heaven. These markers were reminders to the people of God's grace and sustaining care.

We also need markers to follow during our wilderness experiences of discerning God's call in our lives, since discernment often means venturing into unexplored places that are unmapped, unsettled and unfriendly. Whether it is the experience of being in the fog or walking into the desert of Death Valley, wilderness experiences are times when we wander around trying to figure out a way to safety.

The Call of Order in the Midst of Chaos

From my struggles to help Elizabeth listen to what her life was calling her to do and become, I have come to understand that we unknowingly act out the Exodus plot of "wandering in the wilderness" during our discernment process, since we do not know where we are headed. If we can locate the markers of life to us help frame our experience, then we can find new directions for life by rewriting our internal plots to create new stories.

Discernment

Listening to and following a life's calling is another way of talking about discerning God's will for our lives. So often we search for God's will as if we were looking for clues to solve a mystery like the Mystery Inc. gang in an episode of *Scooby-Doo, Where Are You?* Unlike the way that "those meddling kids" solve mysteries by unmasking the villain at the end of every episode, discerning God's will requires an internal process to unmask the hidden questions of our vocation to determine what kind of life God is calling us to live.

In the Q.U.E.S.T.$_{TM}$ to discern God's will, several people have shared their disappointment with me that God does not use social media and post to our computers, tablets, or smart phones. It would be a lot easier in our search for God's calling, the thinking goes, if God sent e-mail and text messages.

Not only does God not use such methods to communicate to us, but He does not even leave detailed operating instructions for our lives. Instead, in order to hear God's voice, we have to learn to read the clues by paying attention to our lives and our experiences. At such a time, we may be encouraged with French philosopher and Jesuit priest Pierre Teilhard de Chardin's advice to his cousin in her time of discernment:

> Above all trust in the slow work of God. We are, quite naturally, impatient in everything to reach the end without delay. We should like to skip the intermediate stages. We are impatient of being on the way to something unknown, something new. And yet it is the law of all progress that it is made by passing through some stages of instability—and it may take a very long time.[6]

This suggests that discernment has to do with our efforts to listen carefully for the voice of vocation so that we can learn to recognize it and follow where it is leading. But how do we recognize our true calling?

When we consider important choices in love or work, what criteria do we use to discern whether or not we are in tune with our calling, with the inner voice, with God's will for us? How do we tell the difference between the authentic voice of vocation and other voices and influences

The Call of Order in the Midst of Chaos

that might confuse us and lead us away from the path that best embodies who we are meant to be?

Over the years, I have discovered there are some obvious pieces to this discernment process, such as adopting a serious attitude about our internal life and searching for ways to deepen it on a regular basis, a willingness to listen to God through the events and people in our lives and to avoid being upset if these things do not seem to be leading us to where we think they should, and a certain amount of courage to make a move and take the logical next step.

We will not get anywhere if we are too timid, too cautious, or too afraid of where it all might lead. Being prudent is one thing; being change-resistant is another. A key element in discerning a calling is to have another person who will listen to give us honest feedback and provide observations that will help us see things more clearly. And as we will see in Chapter Four, the beginning elements of our callings happen to us very early in our lives—often in simple ways that we never would have imagined would lead to a calling.

Questions
1. When considering the important choices in your life, what criteria have you used to discern whether or not you are in tune with your calling?

The Q.U.E.S.T. for Vocation

2. How do you know when you are on the right track? What kinds of feelings do you experience when you are living in tune with your calling?

3. How do you know when you are not? What are the signs that you may be living at odds with yourself?

Notes

1. Frederick Buechner. Wishful Thinking: A Theological ABC. (New York: Harper & Row, 1973).

2. When working with a college student during the process of discerning a life's calling, I respect his or her worldview that he or she brings to the session. For instance, if a student has a Christian perspective, then in my work with him or her, I will use stories from the Bible and Christian tradition. If, however, a student comes to me without a faith perspective, then I will use stories from popular culture, literature, and films.

3. Robert J. Nash and Michele C. Murray. Helping College Students Find Purpose: The Campus Guide to Meaning-Making. (San Francisco: Jossey Bass, Inc. 2010).

4. The wilderness is an in-between place where ordinary life is suspended, identity shifts, and new possibilities emerge. The Hebrew word for wilderness has the dual meaning of both "a desolate and deserted place," as well as "that which is beyond." Through the stories about the Israelites' experiences in exile, we are introduced to the paradoxical nature of the wilderness. It is a place of danger, temptation, and chaos, and a place for solitude, nourishment, and revelation from God. Since most of us imagine the wilderness as a

forest today, I will use wilderness and deep dark forest interchangeably.

5. Genesis 1:2.

6. Pierre Teilhard de Chardin to his cousin Marguerite Teilhard-Chambon, July 4, 1915 in The Making of a Mind.

CHAPTER FOUR

The Call from Childhood Fascinations
ঙ

While no one is expected to leap tall buildings in a single bound, our aspiring heroes will be tested on their courage, integrity, self-sacrifice, compassion and resourcefulness—the stuff of all true superheroes.
—Stan Lee[1]

But now thus says the Lord, he who created you, O Jacob, he who formed you, O Israel: "Fear not, for I have redeemed you; I have called you by name; you are mine."
—Isaiah 43:1

Our earliest passions serve as key indicators of our life's calling. The activities that we participated in as children that seemed to have a timeless quality to them so that we lost sense of time helped to form the beginnings of a calling. Much of this process begins in childhood with associations with heroes, heroines, and often imaginary companions who support us.

The Call from Childhood Fascinations

For instance, at an early age, arithmetic and numbers came easy for my wife, Dionne, and by seventh grade she knew that she was destined to do something with numbers when she grew up. Today she works with numbers as a CPA responsible for corporate income tax compliance.

Ever since she can remember, Pam has always wanted to help others. When asked why she chose her profession as a nephrology nurse, she is quick to say that for her, it was a calling. She states:

> I enjoy caring for kidney-failure patients. I have done a variety of nursing over the years, but was always drawn back to caring for dialysis patients.
>
> Sometimes, dialysis patients get treated like the "underdog." I feel someone needs to be in the underdog's corner, so I support them. I work to educate the community on kidney failure prevention. I could not imagine doing any other type of nursing. My patients give me back as much as I give them. They enrich my life and I hope I make their lives a little easier by providing information they need to make knowledgeable choices in order to live a productive and quality life.

David grew up reading baseball box scores, the statistical summaries of individual and team game performance, from the newspapers. Each day he would write down the stats that told the narrative of each game, create a summary based on the box scores, and then sell this script to others who did not receive a paper. His love for baseball gave way to his lifelong calling of reading and writing to help others to make meaning. David went on to become an English professor.

Dionne's, Pam's, and David's stories are examples of how important elements of our sense of calling can often be traced to the formative influences that certain crucial events, experiences, and persons have had on the direction of our lives. Other times these events that hint at a life's calling will include the imagination of a child's playing with toys, role playing, and a fascination with cartoons.

An Imaginary Friend

When I was a child, I had an imaginary friend that I created out of my baby pillow. I called him *Kick-Kick Batcho*. For years, I kept Kick-Kick a secret from outsiders because I thought other people would ridicule me if they knew he existed. But in my solitude, I would talk with him as if he really were another little child sitting or standing beside me.

I remember that some of the most "serious" decisions I made as a child, such as never having other kindergarteners laugh at my drawings, were formulated under Kick-Kick's guidance. In the same way that the boy from *The Velveteen Rabbit*[2] played with the rabbit, I would call to Kick-Kick, and he would call to me; I would laugh or cry with him; he

The Call from Childhood Fascinations

would laugh or cry with me. There was no doubt in my mind that Kick-Kick was the best friend that I would ever have.

Similarly to the *Peanuts* character Linus's blue blanket, Kick-Kick was my "security blanket"[3] that I carried around with me everywhere I went when I was a child. Using Kick-Kick in a *Calvin and Hobbes*-like fashion helped me make sense out of a world that seemed to be teeming with life at every turn. He was my natural way of being in the world.

As I grew older and, of course, wiser in the judgment of others, I realized that Kick-Kick was not real at all, but rather an alter-ego and companion structured out of my childhood needs and imaginings. In many ways, Kick-Kick was my first understanding of a benevolent God who loved me unconditionally and helped my childhood faith to develop.

Continuing through childhood and adolescence, much of my need for the physical presence of Kick-Kick that was embodied in my baby pillow faded, and I was left with only the *voice*. Everything else had faded or been dismissed from my awareness, but Kick-Kick's voice still remained. To this day, I have learned to pay attention to the voice as he still calls; he still instructs laughs, cries, and reprimands. He still speaks and guides me through life as in folklore a mentor guides a hero during his or her adventure. I still rely on Kick-Kick in a very "real" way.

The Hero/Heroine's Journey

In many ways, Kick-Kick also served as my first image of a hero. I even drew a hero's mask on him, placed a large "K" on his chest, and tied a blue handkerchief around his neck, and began calling him "Super-Kick." A hero/heroine is often considered to be someone born with outstanding ability, courage, and bravery.

Some heroes/heroines have forged their strength and character through their experiences. Their bravery and courage are developed in spite of fear and human failings. For instance, in *The Wizard of Oz*[4] Dorothy must travel with her companions to develop qualities of courage, heart, and thinking before she can return home with a new appreciation for her loved ones. And in the classic 1997 film *Titanic*[5], Rose must learn to take hold of her own life and make it truly her own.

Television has its share of action heroes and battles between the good guys and the bad guys. Many artists have depicted the hero/heroine's journey as a great battle with evil or a quest for something sacred that will help their community. Other heroes must complete a bigger-than-life task. In recent years, Hollywood has capitalized on this notion, as several of the comic-book superheroes sagas have found their way to the silver screen, including Spider-Man, the X-Men, Batman, Superman, the Fantastic Four, the Incredible Hulk, Iron Man, Captain America, Thor, Daredevil, and the Avengers.

The Call from Childhood Fascinations

Even children's cartoons have taken advantage of the superhero craze, as seen from an episode of *SpongeBob SquarePants* in which Patrick Star becomes a superhero. In a scene where Patrick struggles to find his life's calling, he accidentally steps on a Mermaid Man action figure and states:

> I got to figure out what to do with my life. Oh, I wish I was a superhero. That's it. I know what I want to do with my life...at last, I have found my calling: I am Patrick-Man—defender of Bikini Bottom.[6]

Patrick spends the remainder of this episode as a colorful superhero attempting to right the wrongs of evil-doers. As fate would have it, Patrick continues to upset the citizens of Bikini Bottom with his non-heroic missteps and antics. He finally gives up his mask and cape and returns to his rock to wait for the next adventure.

The Call of the Comic Book

Like scores of children, I have spent countless hours following the adventures of a legion of superheroes. This devotion to superheroes created a lifelong passion for fairy tales, biblical stories, cultural myths, folk stories, cartoons, and comic books. My love affair with superheroes first began when I entered second grade, where I met Chad, who introduced me to *Marvel Comics* and the superhero characters who came to life from the cheap pulp pages of comic books.[7]

Using the stories from the comics as a framework, I created a modern-day mythology—where conflict, usually depicted between the hero and a foe in the comics—that would later serve to provide insight for my own struggles in life. These were new myths to me, ones whose stories placed emphasis on color and simplified forms, unlike the hero stories of Hercules, Sinbad, Gulliver, and Robin Hood that were more familiar to me.

From that first moment when I read *The Fantastic Four*, Marvel's first family—which was similar to the families that I knew, who quarreled and held grudges against one another but stuck together in times of crisis—I felt a deep connection to the comic book stories of superheroes. These stories were speaking directly to me and awakened something deep within me. My favorite superhero was the Incredible Hulk, the gigantic, green, irradiated mutant human-monster with incredible strength and size who could not control his rage.

Much of my childhood and current engagement with the Hulk focused on his impulsive, emotional, cunning, brilliant, and scheming ability to be paradoxically both Dr. Bruce Banner's alter-ego and a comic book anti-hero. For me, Hulk is more than just a misunderstood monster; he represents the universal pattern of the *hero/heroine's journey*.

The hero/heroine's journey is a basic pattern that, its proponents argue, is found in many narratives from around the world. In his book *The Hero with a Thousand Faces*, the American scholar of mythology Joseph Campbell holds that numerous myths from various times and regions all share fundamental structures and stages, which he summarizes thus:

> A hero ventures forth from the world of common day into a region of supernatural wonder: fabulous forces are there encountered, and a decisive victory is won: the hero comes back from this mysterious adventure with the power to bestow boons on his fellow man.[8]

According to Campbell, the hero/heroine begins in the ordinary world of everything he or she knows, and receives a call of adventure to enter an unknown world of strange powers and events. Initially, the hero is reluctant and refuses the call until a mentor helps him to get past the initial obstacles. The hero/heroine who eventually accepts the call to enter this strange world must face difficult tasks and trials, either alone or with assistance.

In the most intense versions of the narrative, the heroine must survive a severe challenge, often with help. If she survives, then she may achieve a great gift or "boon." The heroine must then decide whether or not to return to the ordinary world with this boon. If the heroine does decide to return, then she often faces challenges on the return journey. If she returns successfully, then the boon or gift may be used to improve the world. The mythical stories of Osiris (the Egyptian god who was the merciful judge of the dead in the afterlife), Prometheus (the Greek Titan who stole fire from the gods to create civilization), as well as the biblical stories of Moses, Sarah, Ruth, and Deborah, for example, all follow this structure closely.

Campbell describes three sections along this journey: *Call to Adventure*, *Initiation*, and *Return*. The "call to adventure" is the internal urge to begin the Q.U.E.S.T.$_{TM}$ The appearance of the call provides the first step into tension: will the hero accept the call? The call may be a gradual realization, or it may be from a cataclysmic event, such as the destruction of one's home (typically by the villain), or a serious illness. "Initiation" deals with the road of trials during a series of personal tests, tasks, or ordeals that the hero must undergo to begin the transformation. Often the person fails one or more of these tests, which typically occur in threes. "Return" deals with the hero's return home with knowledge and powers acquired on the journey.

Superheroes and a Calling

Over the years, I have spent hours trying to understand my own calling by using the superhero characters from

The Call from Childhood Fascinations

the *Marvel Comics* universe as a pattern. Using the large collection of several (actually close to eighty and growing) superhero action figures in my office, I realized that a lot of the comic book stories of origin were similar to the developmental issues of adults in general and college students in particular.[9]

During several pastoral counseling sessions, in my role as chaplain, I have assisted individuals to select fictional stories that highlight similar issues that they have been facing. The success of using stories to help people find meaning has persuaded me to begin working with superhero action figures with college students to help them discover their life's calling.[10] Similar to sand play therapy[11], the creative process of using miniature figurines in a sand tray to help paint a picture of a person's internal struggle, my process uses the superhero action figure as a catalyst to help students discover the call to deeper meaning.

The idea behind this approach is to allow a student the ability to create a comic book story in which the superhero deals with the student's personal struggle through his imagination. Usually, the student will not realize why he is choosing the action figure he chooses. This becomes apparent, however, when he begins to compare his life with the story of the heroes that he finds appealing. In the process, he is able to translate a personal struggle into a concrete, three-dimensional form to express feelings and conflicts that previously had no verbal language.

Chuck's Story

Chuck was a political science major on full academic scholarship. He was struggling with never having known his father. After listening to his laments about his father's absence, I asked him to tell me about any characters from movies, books, plays, or stories with whom he strongly identified. Immediately he enthusiastically mentioned that since childhood he had had a fascination with Spider-Man.

As he began to explain his connection to Spider-Man, I handed him a Spider-Man action figure and asked him to play with it during our time together. I invited him to select any other action figure that he felt the need to use while determining how Spider-Man would handle his struggle, as if his story were a plot in the comic book.

Chuck began to discuss how he related to Spider-Man's mantra of "with great power comes great responsibility." When asked what this mantra meant to him, he responded,

> What it means? I haven't thought about it much. I just feel like I haven't done enough. I mean, this college has given me a full scholarship, and I feel like I owe it to the college to give back somehow. Power and responsibility are like the urges that I've always had. I guess that it's sort of like a calling. It drives me to use my political

The Call from Childhood Fascinations

science degree and my passion for social justice to help others. I just don't know how to accomplish this.

After a few meetings with me, Chuck realized that behind the action-packed sequences of Spider-Man swinging from tall buildings to capture villains is really his story: the story of a boy looking for his father and, in the process, finding himself. Searching for a missing piece in his life, Chuck began to embody the Spider-Man story.

Much like Peter Parker, who has no parents, Chuck filled his void of an absentee parent with Spider-Man. Chuck's preoccupation with Spider-Man eventually helped him to answer his life's calling to social justice. Through the trial and error process of working in internships at several community development organizations after graduation, Chuck met several like-minded people. One of those individuals asked Chuck about where he saw himself in five years and what type of work he would like to be involved with. Chuck took inventory of his life experiences, including his notion of power and responsibility and his affinity for social justice to help others, and became interested in working full-time for non-profit organizations that specialized in community development. He now works for a non-profit agency that specializes in multi-ethnic public policy research and advocacy. Chuck embodies what it means to have great power and great

The Q.U.E.S.T. for Vocation

responsibility by discovering how to live out his passion for social justice and the study of political science.

Questions
1. My experiences with Kick-Kick and being introduced to Marvel superhero comic books were both important formative experiences for me. Are there particular events or experiences that come to mind that have had an impact on the way your life has unfolded?

2. In what moments, activities, and life experiences have you felt most in touch with your authentic self, your true self, the "real you"? With what kinds of people do you feel most able to be yourself with?

3. Are there activities or events from your childhood that you vividly recall like a scene in a movie? Take a moment to recall these pivotal, formative moments in your life to help you identify an important key to your life's calling.

Notes
1. Peter Sanderson. *Marvel Universe*. (New York: Abradale Press, 2000).

2. Margery Williams and illustrated by William Nicholson. The Velveteen Rabbit. (New York: Avon Books, Inc., 1975).

3. Kick-Kick was my comfort or what pediatrician and psychoanalyst Donald W. Winnicott called a "transitional object" that I used to provide emotional and psychological comfort as I thought that I was a social "misfit" and no one understood me because of my vivid

The Call from Childhood Fascinations

imagination. D.W. Winnicott. Playing and Reality, (London: Tavistock Publication Ltd., 1971).

4. The Wizard of Oz. Dir. Victor Fleming. Perf. Judy Garland, Ray Bolger, Jack Haley, Bert Lahr, and Frank Morgan. Metro-Goldwyn-Mayer, 1939. Film.

5. Titanic. Dir. James Cameron. Perf. Leonardo DiCaprio and Kate Winslet. Paramount Pictures and 20th Century Fox, 1997. Film.

6. "Patrick-Man." SpongeBob SquarePants. Nickelodeon. 27 Oct. 2012. Television.

7. From the humble beginnings during the Depression, costing only a dime, the superhero comic book is essentially a familiar concept in a new package, since throughout history human beings have been fascinated with stories about godlike and heroic figures.

8. Joseph Campbell. The Hero with a Thousand Faces, (New York: Pantheon Books, 1949).

9. Much as the plot of an origin story of the superhero struggling to integrate his or her newly found powers with an existing identity, college student development begins with establishing an identity in a new world and moves toward developing purpose and integrity. The next stage of development is developing competence, which is followed by managing emotions, moving through the stages of autonomy and interdependence to develop mature relationships. See Arthur W. Chickering and Linda Reisser. Education and Identity, (San Francisco: John Wiley & Sons, 1993).

10. Lawrence C. Rubin. Editor. Using Superheroes in Counseling and Play Therapy, (Springer Publishing Company: New York, 2007).

11. Developed by Jungian therapist Dora Kalff in the 1950s and '60s based on her studies at the C.G. Jung Institute, Zurich, sand play therapy is an expressive and dynamic play process that is used by children, adolescents, individual adults, couples, families and groups. An individual is given the possibility, by means of figures and the arrangement of the sand in the area bounded by the sandbox, to set up a world corresponding to his or her inner state. In this manner, through free, creative play, unconscious processes are made visible in a three-dimensional form and a pictorial world comparable to the dream experience.

CHAPTER FIVE

The Call of a New Self-Image
☯

Before you tell your life what you intend to do with it, listen for what it intends to do with you. Before you tell your life what truths and values you have decided to live up to, let your life tell you what truths you embody, what values you represent.

—Parker J. Palmer [1]

So if anyone is in Christ, there is a new creation: everything old has passed away; see, everything has become new!

—2 Corinthians 5:17

In the previous chapter, Chuck learned that when something goes wrong in life, such as never having known our father, our self-image is affected in a drastic way. We are called to go on a Q.U.E.S.T.$_{TM}$ to find a way for whatever is wrong with our lives to be fixed. In a similar way to Chuck's story, the biblical character Naaman[2] answers the call of the Q.U.E.S.T$_{TM}$ to find a new self-image. Naaman's

The Q.U.E.S.T. for Vocation

Q.U.E.S.T.$_{TM}$ focuses on finding relief from a disease that threatens to strip him of his identity.

Naaman is the chief commander of the king of Syria's army. He is an honorable and mighty leader. After a successful battle against Israel, Naaman returns home with increased grandeur and the booty of war, including a young Israelite girl as captive. But that is not all: Naaman is also stricken by leprosy.

The remedy for Naaman comes from an unlikely source: the captive Israelite girl, who tells him about the wonder-working prophet in Israel: Elisha. Desperate to be healed, even though it means entering the enemy territory of Israel, Naaman believes the girl. He goes to the Syrian king, who writes a letter to his Israelite enemy about his beloved commander, saying, "Please cure my servant Naaman." Armed with the appeal letter from the king of Syria, as well as with lots of money and gifts, Naaman leaves for Israel in an attempt to buy a cure.

When Naaman arrives in Israel, the king of Israel is afraid that this is a trick to restart the fighting, and he does not know what to do. The situation is a bizarre one: a hostile pagan king asking an impossible favor for his generalissimo, who has killed the previous Israelite king. This sets the stage for disappointment and what might well be the next political disaster: "Just look," says the king of Israel, "and see how he is trying to pick a quarrel with me."

The Call of a New Self-Image

Elisha, the prophet, hears about the dilemma and tells the king to send Naaman to him.

When Naaman gets to Elisha's home, Elisha is not impressed by his power and money and does not come out to meet him; rather, he just tells him how to be healed: go to the Jordan River and bathe seven times. Naaman reluctantly follows these unconventional directions for a cure. He emerges from the Jordan healed of his disease, and his self-image is instantly changed.

Searching for a New Self-Image

No matter whether we suffer from a chronic disease or we are in excellent health, we all have some type of self-image. For many of us, our self-image is determined by early life experiences and the opinion of others. But the origin of our self-image is often unknown to us and goes unexamined.

Like Naaman's painful self-image of being a leper and his assumption that he should be cured, we all have a self-image that assumes a certain right to be healthy. But what happens when our health fails?

For most of us, moving from a self-understanding that assumes good health to the devastating news that we are not healthy is a serious blow to our self-image. When this occurs, it becomes important to pay attention to the transitory nature of the "identity mask[3]" that we carve out for ourselves to wear. When we experience an unexpected loss, our identity mask begins to crack, forcing us to answer the call of discovering our true nature.

Developing a Professional Identity

And as we discovered from Chuck's story in the previous chapter, every calling begins with discovering our identity by answering the questions such as: *"What has my life been trying to do with me?"*, *"What has my life been preparing me for?"*, and *"Who is my life calling me to become?"* Like most professionals, I have spent much of my energy busily building an identity mask to give me status and satisfaction in the work world.

Because this mask had served me well, I was conscious of only part of this mask. But other parts of my identity mask were hidden from my awareness, and these began to point to insights into my life's calling. I was naïve about how my life's calling would include *all* of my experiences—including how my ethnicity would shape my identity mask. Discerning the hidden elements that produced this mask requires going back into my personal history.

Part of my current mask or professional self-image consists of being one of only a few United Methodist clergy who have graduated from both United Methodist seminaries in Georgia: The Candler School of Theology at Emory

University and The Interdenominational Theological Center at Gammon Seminary, both in Atlanta, Georgia.

Having advanced degrees from both institutions has been an important part of my identity over the years. Historically, Gammon Seminary, known as the "School of the Prophets," with its long-standing tradition of great orators and fiery preachers, has been the seminary where many Black[4] United Methodist ministers have chosen to pursue theological training.

The line of thinking that I have heard from some of the Gammon alumni clergy goes: "If Gammon is the school of the prophets, then Candler at Emory must be the 'School of the Scribes,' which places its emphasis not on preaching, but on the importance of scholarly understanding and the interpretation of the biblical text."

Following this line of thinking, which is a gross overgeneralization, Candler became known to many Blacks as the chosen place where the "majority" of United Methodist persons prepare for ministry and Gammon became the place where "minorities," especially a large number of Black United Methodists, prepare.

While enrolled at Candler, I applied for a scholarship that was awarded to Black students who demonstrated academic excellence and a commitment to service and community engagement. During the interview with the selection committee, I was told by a Black non-Candler faculty committee member that I was not "Black" enough. Taken aback by his condescending critique, I surmised that he meant what I had heard from several others who had taken the mantle of being the arbiter of all things black: "Ok, so he looks black, and he kind of does the 'black' thing, but he's not really down with the 'black' cause. He's not one of us. He just ain't 'black' enough."

I did not receive the scholarship, and the irony of the whole encounter was that my skin complexion was actually two shades darker than his! But it was not funny at the time. His statement struck a nerve that became the driving factor to prove that I *was* "Black enough," which eventually led to my desire to create a professional identity mask that was socially acceptable—especially among my own people.

Racial Identity Development

In crafting this professional identity mask, I remained unaware of the power of the racial elements that I was wearing along with this mask. Many of the racial elements that I had unconsciously incorporated in my professional identity mask had been passed down to me by older clergy through anecdotal stories of the mistreatment of Blacks during the dissolving of the Central Jurisdiction[5], the all-Black clergy conference that was dismantled in 1968.

Reflecting on these stories and my experiences, I now recognize that a large part of my unconscious professional

The Call of a New Self-Image

self-image of graduating from Candler and Gammon began during my high school years of trying to establish what Christian mystic Howard Thurman calls a "healthy sense of self."[6]

The Wake-up Call

In 1986, when I was a junior in high school at East Hall High School, I experienced a startling encounter that served as a wake-up call and that prompted the questioning of my sense of self-worth. Every morning the students on my school bus, who were all Black, were greeted by the Ku Klux Klan, fully robed with hoods, parading across the street of the school on private property. These events were surprising, as our school did not seem to have any racial tensions. The only tension that we knew of was with the rival city high school that we rallied against to prove that we were not the "country bumpkins" that they often called us.

We could not understand what anyone in our school could have done to provoke the Klan to parade in front of our school. Seeing the Klan fully robed, we assumed that they were present because of something that we had done, since this was the prevailing assumption held by many Blacks from the time of Jim Crow and the sinister experiences of the Klan marching and burning crosses to intimidate others. At least, this had been the story that our parents had passed down to us of their experiences with the Klan.

The Q.U.E.S.T. for Vocation

We never did find out why the Klan was at our school. We were just grateful that there was not a violent confrontation between students because of their presence. But that encounter left an indelible mark on my psyche that would haunt me continually, as their presence was a painful reminder to me that not everyone could see beyond skin color.

I was changed by this unwelcomed and unsuspecting experience. No matter how much I tried to block out the experience, by pretending that it did not happen so that I could avoid confronting the ugly nature of prejudice, the image would not go away.

I was an impressionable sixteen-year-old, and I thought the world revolved around me. Like my comic book hero the Incredible Hulk, I lacked the ability to control my anger and rage. And after this encounter with the Klan, I grew suspicious of any person who was not Black, even if he or she had good intentions. Though unknown to me at the time, this experience was akin to what Beverly Tatum calls "the encounter stage" of the Racial Identity Development Theory[7], in which an encounter, or series of encounters, forces us to acknowledge the impact of racism on our lives.

What a difference a year made! By my senior year, under the strong influence of my parents and relatives who had experienced racism and Jim Crow but found the inner strength and faith to move past racial prejudice, I was eventually able to work through my anger and rage.

The Call of a New Self-Image

During my senior year, my American History teacher asked me to teach a section on Black History to the class. She mentioned that to her knowledge, this was the first time that the topic had ever been taught by a student. The praises that I received from my peers for the open and honest discussions about American history, the Civil Rights Movement, and race relations were the beginnings of a call to a peace-making approach to race relations. The experience also helped me to become less suspicious of others.

Reviewing these high school experiences helped me to see what motivated me to attend both seminaries: my need to be accepted. Those early experiences of race relations helped to forge a call for me to seek internal peace. My need to be an integral part of the so-called "Black experience" became so strong that a few years after I graduated from Candler, I enrolled at Gammon to pursue a doctoral degree.

Influenced by the Gammon tradition being the "School of Prophets," I reckoned that my education there would teach me to practice ministry, proclaim God's justice and peace, and ultimately quench my thirst to understand the cultural differences between Black and White culture. Little did I know that taking classes as a doctoral student while continuing to work full-time would take its toll on me mentally, physically, and emotionally. It was not long before it became difficult for me to keep up with the constant rigor of classes. I quickly forgot about my desire

The Q.U.E.S.T. for Vocation

to understand cultural differences as I did not have time to think about anything else but working, studying, and trying to find a few hours for sleeping.

At times, this cycle was so intense that I neglected my body. I picked up poor eating habits and did not get enough sleep during those years. I was so consumed with reading, studying, and writing papers that I did not even know that I was sick during the bulk of my time at Gammon. Nor could I imagine that seven months after graduation, I would be on nightly dialysis that would lead to a physical calling from my body.

Questions
1. I had several formative experiences that seemed to be disconnected and random but when I began to pay attention to them turned out to be part of a larger calling. What are the seemingly disconnected and random experiences in your life trying to tell you?

2. Removing an identity mask exposes us to questions of self-image. Have you had experiences when you were forced to remove your identity mask?

3. My experiences of race relations forged a desire to be accepted by others. What are the experiences in your life that drive your need to be accepted?

Notes
1. Parker Palmer. Let Your Life Speak: Listening to Voice of Vocation, (San Francisco: JosseyBass, 2000).

The Call of a New Self-Image

2. Naaman's story can be found in 2 Kings 5:1-19.

3. An "identity mask" is a term used to describe specific social and professional roles. It is identical to the psychological notion of the "persona," which consists of the mask or appearance that we present to the world. For Swiss psychologist Carl Jung, it is the social face that the individual presents to the world—a kind of mask, designed on the one hand to make a definite impression upon others, and on the other to conceal the true nature of the individual. According to Jung, problems occur when we identify with the persona or identity mask so that we believe that that persona is the totality of who we are, and we have little or no concept of ourselves as distinct from what society expects of us. See C. G. Jung, Memories, Dreams, Reflections. (New York: Random House, Inc, 1963).

4. I intentionally use the word "Black" instead of "African-American," even though the term "African-American" is politically correct. My wife's family is of West Indian descent (i.e., from the Caribbean). In order to include her and her family in my conversations, I have stopped using the term "African-American," since they are of African descent but are not American.

5. The Central Jurisdiction (the all-Black, segregated conference of the Methodist Episcopal Church) was established in 1939 with the merger of the Methodist Episcopal Church, the Methodist Episcopal Church South, and the Methodist Protestant Church. It was eliminated by action of the 1968 General Conference when the Methodist Church merged with the Evangelical United Brethren Church in Dallas, Texas. The Central Jurisdiction was a way that the church avoided

integration. See Peter C. Murray. Methodists and the Crucible of Race, 1930-1975, (Columbia: University of Missouri Press, 2004).

6. According to Howard Thurman, the self (or the personal) is concerned with questions of integrity that begin with identity and purpose and move towards the social (or public) dimension of life. This involves the relationship with the other and finally the spiritual, which addresses the human need for excellence, hope, and a sense of the ultimate. All of these movements create a sense of wholeness, a sense of community within self, or "a healthy sense of self," which is the basis upon which one's unique potential and self-worth is understood. Howard Thurman. With Head and Heart: The Autobiography of Howard Thurman. (Orlando: Harcourt Brace & Company, 1979).

7. Beverly Daniel Tatum. *Why Are All the Black Kids Sitting Together in the Cafeteria? And Other Conversations about Race*. (New York: Basic Books, 1997).

Part Two

The Physical Call from the Body

CHAPTER SIX

The Call to Enter the Unknown
ಡ

Stick to the forest-track, keep your spirits up, hope for the best, and with a tremendous slice of luck you may come out one day and see the Long Marshes lying below you, and beyond them, high in the East, the Lonely Mountain where dear old Smaug lives, though I hope he is not expecting you.

—Gandalf[1]

So that, with the eyes of your heart enlightened, you may know what is the hope to which he has called you, what are the riches of his glorious inheritance among the saints, and what is the immeasurable greatness of his power for us who believe, according to the working of his great power.

—Ephesians 1:18-19

Jack Frost, one of the fictional characters in *The Rise of the Guardians*[2], the animated epic film that tells the story of identity and purpose, is instructive in beginning a chapter on answering the call to enter the unknown. Jack does not know why he exists. He knows only that he is

The Q.U.E.S.T. for Vocation

Jack Frost, and he is nagged by a past life that he intuitively knows about but cannot remember. As the personification of cold weather who is held responsible for nipping at the nose and toes, coloring the foliage in autumn, and leaving fernlike patterns on cold windows, Jack Frost is re-imaged in the film as a teen-aged boy. He is frustrated with the Man in the Moon for never answering his questions of identity and purpose.

Jack is invited to become a *Guardian of Childhood*, but he refuses. Another guardian, North, the film's Santa Claus character, takes Jack to his inner workshop, where he shares his prized toys made of ice. Showing his massive display of toys, North asks Jack to reconsider being a Guardian. Jack asks, "Why me?" North responds, "You have something very special inside, and we can't do it without you."

North gives Jack a Santa Claus version of a Russian nesting doll, one of those sets of wooden dolls of decreasing size placed one inside the other, and he explains that the dolls represent the different faces of Santa. When Jack reaches the center doll, he finds a baby version of Santa with large eyes. He comments on the large eyes, and North responds by saying, "They are eyes of wonder.... Every Guardian must discover for him- or herself, their center. This is my center. I see wonder in everything. My center is to bring wonder to the world."

The Call to Enter the Unknown

North asks Jack, "Who are you, Jack? What is your center?" Jack does not answer. He has memories—a past before he became Frost—but he cannot penetrate the icy sheet that has masked his memories.

Intrigued with the promise to help him recover his previous life's memories, Jack decides to join the Guardians to fight off the villain, Pitch, a boogeyman character of the film. Along the way, Jack begins hearing a voice calling him by name. Recognizing the voice, he follows it into a deep, dark forest and begins his Q.U.E.S.T.$_{TM}$ for a life's calling to discover his true identity and reason for being.

In many ways, Jack Frost's Q.U.E.S.T.$_{TM}$ to discover his center is a modern-day fairy tale, such as "Snow White and the Seven Dwarfs"[3] as told by the German folklorists the Brothers Grimm, in which the central character is often called by some urge beyond his or her knowing, to journey into the deep, dark forest in search of something that he or she has lost and to face his or her worst fears. Recall how in Walt Disney's 1937 animated version of the fairy tale, Snow White flees into the dark forest, on the way to the dwarf cottage, and her terrified imagination turns ordinary trees into threatening demons.

Like Jack Frost and Snow White, when we answer a call, we embark on a journey in which we leave behind the world we have always known for the pathless and fearful world of the unknown. In many stories, the characters often know nothing—where they will go, how they will eat, who will support them, or where they will end up.

The pattern of answering a calling in fairy tales is instructive for us in discerning our life's calling. In most fairy tales, the dark forest, like the wilderness, and the watery chaos of the "deep" from the creation story discussed in Chapter Three, is a repetitive theme that signifies the unknown, where the wild things live. It is in the forest of fairy tales that we meet frog princes, wise old men, a golden goose, a ravenous wolf, imposing giants, spirit messengers, and all manner of creatures that help the protagonist learn the valuable lesson of becoming more self-aware.

In a similar way, in our search for a life's calling, the dark forest serves as a metaphor that represents the depths of our being: the place where our instincts, full knowing, and true nature live. When we walk into the dark forest, we step into a world full of adventure, trepidation, challenges and unpredictability.

By entering this space, we are "sinking into our innermost nature" and finding out what it feels like to live from that space; we are literally in the process of being born anew from our inner essence. From there we can listen more intently to our calling and approach our problems from a different perspective. This enables us to resolve our current issues as well as to reconnect with ourselves and others more fully.

In the fall, while I was in the second year of my doctoral studies, I was distressed from the lack of balance among my home, work, and school life. At the same time, I was also grieving for the loss of my favorite restaurant. It turns out that what I was grieving for was something far greater than a work-life balance and the bricks and mortar of a restaurant.

The Vacant Lot

I entered the "dark forest" unexpectedly by simply walking aimlessly around a vacant lot. Each day, I would shuffle through dirt, kick an occasional aluminum can, and side-step mud puddles that transformed the barren lot into "moon craters." Although I was uncharacteristically out of breath during my blind ritual, I kept circling around the remaining footprint of Tyler's Restaurant in LaGrange, Georgia, as if I were walking a labyrinth, hoping for divine intervention.

At the time, circling the vacant lot seemed like a good way to mourn the loss of my favorite breakfast restaurant. I suppose that my wandering around the vacant lot was my way of "acting out" the emotions that I did not have the words to express. The struggle to accept that my favorite restaurant had been leveled paved the way to discovering

The Q.U.E.S.T. for Vocation

what had been leveled within me that caused my aimless wandering. Simply put, I was in a major transition that felt as if the fog had rolled in from the San Francisco Bay, and I could not see which direction to move.

Several months after walking around the vacant lot, I continued to have experiences with shortness of breath. I finally went to the doctor for tests and discovered that the cause of my shortness-of-breath episodes was excessive fluid buildup.

The Hawk Encounter

During a follow-up visit to the doctor's office at LaGrange Internal Medicine in LaGrange, Georgia, I had an unlikely encounter with a red-tailed hawk that turned out to be more than an occasional bird crossing my path. One day while I was driving to the doctor's office for an additional laboratory test to determine why I was retaining fluid, a red-tailed hawk flew across my path and startled me. Gathering my composure from a near-miss hawk attack, I entered into the doctor's office for more than two hours of tests.

As I was leaving the doctor's office, I was surprised to see the hawk once again. This time, however, I became curious and drove behind it to follow its flight path. Behaving as if it was calling me to an unknown destination and wanting me to follow along, it flew and landed at the top of a large pine tree near a private high school, a church, and the doctor's office. I pulled onto the shoulder of the state highway, parked, and got out to look at the hawk.

Miraculously, the hawk looked down at me as if it was waiting for me to catch up to it. It fluttered its wings and pointed its head towards the west. I began to wonder if the hawk was trying to communicate with me. Before I could think, I blurted out, "What do you want with me?" Then, in a moment of shame, I looked around when I realized that I was talking to a bird! Stunned by my behavior, I was hoping that nobody that I knew saw me out on the shoulder of the road, looking up into a tree and seemingly talking to myself.

I felt a bit crazy, but I was determined to figure out why this hawk had sought me out. Suddenly, the words "Face the sun" came from a voice from within. I did not know the origin of this statement, as I would not have ever thought it. But when I repeated it out loud, the bird nodded, turned westward, and flew away into the large setting sun. Reminded of the biblical story of Balaam's talking donkey[4], I wondered if God had spoken to me through an animal.

According to the story, Balaam is a head-strong commander who is determined to complete his task. As he is on the way, his donkey begins to act strangely by turning away from the path. Each time the donkey turns from the path, Balaam's leg gets pressed against a wall. Outraged by his donkey's erratic behavior, Balaam repeatedly strikes the donkey. Balaam is unaware of what the donkey sees ahead: an angel armed with a flaming sword, blocking the path.

I am embarrassed to admit that I was as blind and clueless as Balaam. I thought that I knew what was best for me. Due to my theological education, I lived out of my head and was taught to believe in things that I could measure and follow logically. I ignored anything that contradicted this worldview, including the clues from my body suggesting that living exclusively out of my head while ignoring my body and my feelings was destructive. Instead, I pressed on along a dangerous path.

Following the story metaphorically, my body represented Balaam's donkey, and the hawk represented the angel/messenger of God trying to get me to turn in a different direction. And like Balaam's donkey, my body had been acting erratically to get my attention, but I ignored it. My eyes and ears were about to be opened to God's mysterious message that would alter the future direction of my life forever.

Facing the Sun

It took a little over two weeks to get the conclusive results back from my extensive lab work. In the meantime, I tried to make sense of my hawk encounter. I read everything that I could on the behavior patterns of hawks. I even traveled

The Call to Enter the Unknown

to Callaway Gardens in Pine Mountain, Georgia, to attend the Birds of Prey Show, which features a red-tailed hawk demonstration, and I interviewed the hawk trainer. He had no answers to why the hawk would act in this manner, as normally hawks try to stay away from humans.

Not being able to determine the erratic behavior of the hawk, I decided to focus my energy on discerning the internal call to "face the sun." Analyzing the encounter as if it were a waking dream, I made symbolic associations with the west and the setting sun. Over time, I settled on the notion that "Face the sun" was a metaphorical statement that called me to face the direction of chaos—the unknown, darkness, night, and death—since the sun was setting on the day of the hawk encounter.

Armed with the mantra of "facing the sun," I pieced together another way of thinking about it that focused on "facing the Son" of God. Was I was being called to go on a Q.U.E.S.T.$_{TM}$ to experience the Christian notion of suffering, death, and resurrection—the process of suffering to let go of some of my fundamental assumptions about life, illness, faith, and God to be renewed? Only time would tell.

Questions
1. In the film The Rise of the Guardians, Jack Frost has to discover his center by going on a quest to remember his past. Through an epic adventure with other legendary children characters, Jack discovers his center. In what

ways do you identify with Jack's quest for identity and calling?

2. When I was struggling to figure out the source of my failing health, I had to make sense of a strange call to "face the sun." Have you ever had to make sense of a strange calling? If so, how did you make sense of it?

3. During my experience, I was surprised to discover that I had been unconsciously living out Balaam's story by refusing to listen to my body. Have there been times when you ignored your body and had to be stopped in your tracks?

Notes

1. J.R.R. Tolkien. The Hobbit, Or There and Back Again. (London: George Allen & Unwin, 1937).

2. The Rise of the Guardians. Dir. Peter Ramsey. Perf. Chris Pine, Alec Baldwin, and Hugh Jackman. Paramount Pictures, 2012. Film.

3. Jacob Ludwig Carl Grimm and Wilhelm Carl Grimm. Trans. Margaret Hunt. Household Tales by the Brothers Grimm. "Little Snow White." (London: George Bell and Sons, 1884).

4. Numbers 22:22-33.

CHAPTER SEVEN

The Call of the Dark Night of the Soul

ଃ

From the standpoint of the soul, a life-threatening illness is a spiritual journey—an adventure or an ordeal or an initiation—that is undertaken...and can be shared by others. The possibility of losing a sense of meaning as well as losing life are risks for the patient and her companions; the possibility of finding one's soul and living or dying with an I-Thou relationship is the opportunity for both.
—Jean Shinoda Bolen, M.D.[1]

Then Jacob woke from his sleep and said, "Surely the Lord is in this place—and I did not know it." And he was afraid, and said, "How awesome is this place! This is none other than the house of God, and this is the gate of heaven." —Genesis 28:16-17

Cleopas and his friend leave Jerusalem, traveling on the road to the Emmaus village, after witnessing Jesus' death. Distraught from losing the person for whom

The Q.U.E.S.T. for Vocation

they have left everything in order to follow, they believe that he and his cause have been destroyed. Now that he is dead and gone, they are in a state of disorientation. They are not willing to stick around and discuss the meaning of what has happened to Jesus or to hear the good news of his resurrection. They know what has happened. He is dead. The kingdom that they have hoped he had come to found is now a hopeless dream. They think that all his and their efforts have been futile, wasted time, and they lament all the things that have occurred.[2]

The biblical story of the road to Emmaus highlights for us that there is no way to avoid the period of darkness that comes after we have experienced devastating news. It is as if news of this sort serves as an unwelcomed call that pushes us to a difficult place where we are unwilling and unable to go to emotionally. We sink into a depression and cannot respond to the call until we have found a way to accept the difficult news that we have received.

During my next visit to the doctor after the hawk experience, I received the devastating results of my long-awaited lab work. I was suffering from *end-stage kidney disease*[3] due to several years of undiagnosed high blood pressure.

I was helpless, and it was as if a veil had been dropped between me and the rest of the world. The world was continuing on its usual path, people around me were in motion, and I was close enough to see them—but just not

The Call of the Dark Night of the Soul

able to be with them, as it felt as if I were watching alone from a distance. I was in what Christian mystic St. John of the Cross called a "dark night of the soul,"[4] where darkness represented the hardships and emotional difficulties that I was experiencing.

I kept telling myself that the hawk encounter *was* a God-moment calling me. But my efforts to convince myself were not enough to prevent me from doubting God's presence in the difficult times when the weight of my disease was too much for me to bear. One day I would be brimming with the confidence of knowing that God's call was leading me while I walked through the unknown, and on other days—in some cases the very next day—I would feel the total opposite way: overcome with fear and doubting that God had called me at all.

Loss of a Dream

I was blindly following a path similar to the one experienced by Joseph, the biblical dreamer. Joseph, an unpretentious teenager, is the eleventh of the patriarch Jacob's twelve sons. He is unaware of how his dreams are being interpreted by his brothers. Undaunted by how he is perceived, he keeps reporting his dreams. Eventually his brothers grow tired of his dreams, all of which seem to arrogantly portray that he will one day rule over his family.

The Q.U.E.S.T. for Vocation

Upset by his dreams, his brothers sell Joseph into slavery. Joseph's dreams become a nightmare, as he has to suffer from several difficult experiences, including being framed for rape, jailed, and forgotten about and left to perish in a foreign prison.

After my doctor's diagnosis of my kidney disease, I felt as if I had been taken captive by my body and given a prison sentence without the chance of parole. My life was not supposed to be like this. I had plans and dreams to live a happy and healthy life. But just as Joseph does, I kept following my dreams, even though everything around me said to do otherwise.

I was twenty-eight years old, and I was struggling with a call to "face the sun" that seemed to contradict everything that I knew. I was losing grasp on the dream of living a healthy life that was pain free. Up to this point, I had never had a major illness, undergone surgery, or even been admitted to the hospital. Not having had any type of surgery was a badge of honor that I proudly (if not arrogantly) wore on my chest. And just as Joseph's dreams do for him during his teenager years, my badge of health fed into a youthful dream of invincibility that led me to believe that somehow I was healthier than others. My youthful dream was quickly becoming my worst nightmare.

Being a sick person for the rest of my life was not what I had dreamed about in elementary school when I was figuring out what I wanted to do when I grew up. Instead, like most of my friends, I wanted to become something that fed into my youthful sense of invincibility: a football player.

I followed the football path until junior high school, when I quickly discovered that there were other players who were bigger, stronger, faster, and much better than I was. I was forced to find a new dream to help me navigate through life.

According to developmental psychologist Daniel Levinson, the "dream" that I bought into symbolized youth, omnipotence, illusion, inspiration, and heroic drama.[5] Author and theology professor Sharon Daloz Parks adds faith to Levinson's notion of the dream and states:

> A worthy faith must bear the test of lived experience in the real world—our discoveries and disappointments, expectations and betrayals, assumptions and surprises. It is in the ongoing dialogue between self and the world, between community and lived reality, that meaning—a faith—takes form.[6]

I had to learn to ask what Parks calls "big enough" questions to determine a dream with a capital "D" in my search for new meaning, purpose, and faith as my sickness forced me to give up my former "dream." It was hard to accept the loss and disappointment of being ejected from the ranks of the physically unblemished.

Over the next few years of my life, I would struggle with finding a new dream that was not forthcoming. Frustrated without a new dream to pursue, I clung to the dream of being physically healthy. I reluctantly answered the call to begin a Q.U.E.S.T.$_{TM}$ to discover how my dream of health that I was still identifying with had run its course. It was not just my overwhelming health issues that were causing me to waver in fully answering the call. There were other parts of my life that began to unravel and contributed to the emotional pain and darkness that I was experiencing.

Soon after my hawk encounter and diagnosis of kidney disease, I learned that my mother was suffering from an aggressive form of liver cancer. When I heard this, it felt as if I were sinking deeper into the darkness. I grew numb and did everything that I could to hold back the thought that my mother would die. While I was struggling with my mother's cancer and coming to terms with my own illness, my marriage fell apart, due to an on-going affair my wife was having, which ultimately led to separation and then a painful divorce.

Each one of these crises could have easily destroyed any person, but going through all three at once was a triple whammy and could be enough to cause a person to lose faith. I was no different. Within a few months, my entire support system had been leveled like Tyler's Restaurant, and I was left alone in a vacant lot. My faith was crumbling, and

The Call of the Dark Night of the Soul

I felt as if I were in exile, away from God. My "God-box," the framework and worldview that was filled with bits of scriptural wisdom, assumptions of God's nature, and work in my life, was bursting apart at the seams.

An invisible chronic illness[7] had invaded my life and ruined my dreams by bringing with it the agents of chaos in the form of my mother dying from liver cancer and of my going through a difficult divorce. I lost grasp of my dream of well-being and what it meant to be healthy. I began to question what I was going to do in my later years with this invisible chronic illness, and I wondered if it would hinder what I wanted to accomplish with my life.

Eventually the questions waned, and I turned to the Bible to find solace. A new dream emerged. Bible stories of God's grace and care during alienation, displacement and exile provided comfort to me during this time. Revisiting the great biblical stories of crises helped to make my transition from good health to kidney disease a purposeful series of events that would help me to eventually rewrite my life's story, a story in which the protagonist is a person with failing kidneys who would eventually need dialysis and a transplant in order to live.

The Process of Transition

During every crisis, whether we are aware of it or not, we are being called to connect the stories of our lives to a

The Q.U.E.S.T. for Vocation

larger story of meaning and purpose. A crisis is a transition, and contrary to popular belief, a *transition* is not just a nice way to say *change*. Rather, it a process that requires us to *let go of the past, endure limbo*, and *receive a new beginning*.

I first experienced these insights from author and organizational consultant William Bridges via his book *Transitions: Making Sense of Life's Changes*[8], but it was the experiences from my prolonged health struggles that actually confirmed the process. For instance, my vacant lot experience of grieving the loss of Tyler's Restaurant was a good example of the "letting go" phase of transition. And, while unknown to me at the time, the diagnosis of kidney disease and the chaotic emotions that it produced were part of the "limbo" phase of transition.

Struggling to move through this experience of a dark forest that had turned into a vacant lot, I needed a road map to mark my experiences and to help me understand where I had been and where I was going. By happenstance, my road map consisted of a vacant lot and a hawk-guide that called me to the process of *metanoia*.[9]

A Greek word translated as "repentance" in the New Testament, *metanoia* literally means "to go beyond our present state of mind" or "to think differently afterward." It implies a "change of heart and mind" and a redefining or turning of our whole selves—including our faults, strengths, and everything else in between—toward God's grace to discern our life's calling by rewriting our stories. Remembering our stories in the light of God's story invites us to tell our life experiences in light of God's powerful work in human history.

My bizarre hawk encounter and the subsequent news that I was suffering from kidney disease were *metanoia* experiences calling me to turn around and "face the sun." The process of turning around was a slow and painful one. Surprisingly, relief from my pain came to me in an odd way. By replacing my vacant lot experience with the *wilderness* imagery from the Exodus story, in which God leads the people by a roundabout way to the Promised Land, I had glimpses of a much larger perspective on my illness that suggested that I was traveling in the right direction.

According to the story, a band of fugitive slaves has left behind the secure, familiar, but oppressive Egypt. But before they are finally able to cross the river into the new country of promise, they meander through "no-place," traveling in frustrated circles. They wander in the wilderness of "a huge vacant lot" for forty years![10] Somehow this state of wandering aimlessly is necessary for the people to discover who they are as people of God.

Looking back on my wanderings through the vacant lot, I began to see how I was unknowingly following the pattern of the exodus as a make-shift ritual of transition. I

The Q.U.E.S.T. for Vocation

realized that by wandering around a vacant lot, I was following my own modern-day exodus.

Being sidetracked and sometimes wandering in circles looking for my own version of God's "Promised Land," I was looking for hope to relieve my suffering. Along their exodus route, the people are guided by God's presence in the form of a cloud by day and a pillar of fire by night. But I could not see any sign of God's presence or grasp the notion that God was walking alongside me.

I was emotionally stuck and spiritually blind; all that I could feel and see was the emptiness of a vacant lot. I had to let go of my old "Egypt-systems thinking," represented by the life that I was accustomed to before getting sick, in order to get to the Promised Land and to see God walking in the midst of my suffering. Eventually, I was able to see the wilderness of my kidney disease through the lens of the exodus story. I felt that I was no longer just wandering in a vacant lot alone. God was walking beside me guiding me, just as God had done with the people of Israel.

God's walking with me became a "living metaphor," as I had a first-hand experience of what the people of the exodus learn: God can be discovered and trusted in the midst of wilderness wandering. I carried this new insight with me through dialysis, transplantation, and transplant rejection. And I carried it during my return to dialysis while waiting for a second kidney transplant. I finally moved on to the "new beginning" phase of transition with a renewed faith in God, who walks with us through the wilderness experiences of life.

The Tyler's lot is no longer vacant, as a few years ago a bank was built on it. Occasionally, I still walk through the parking lot, reminiscing about how the vacant lot had provided a means for me to come to terms with a difficult time in my life. Over the course of my transition, my faith was shaken, stirred, and poured out again in a new shape. The physical and emotional ordeals that I endured helped me see the need to live for the moment and to trust that God walks alongside me to transform painful moments into something sacred.

Questions
1. Have you ever felt that you were being led or encouraged to move in one direction rather than another or had a life experience like my red-tailed hawk encounter, which seemed to "speak" to you about the direction of your life? What was the message? What was your response?

2. Have you ever thought that God might be calling or speaking to you in a personal way? Recall the experience. What was the message? How did you respond?

3. Author Sharon Parks suggests that vocation is best described as our "Dream with a capital D." I lost my

dream of being a healthy person after my diagnosis of end-stage kidney disease. What is your personal Dream? As you imagine your future, what images come to mind of the kind of life you hope to be leading, the kind of world you would like to be living in or creating?

Notes

1. Jean Shindoa Bolden. Close to the Bone: Life-Threatening Illness and the Search for Meaning. (New York: Touch Stone, 1986).

2. See Luke 24.

3. End-stage kidney disease occurs when the kidneys are no longer able to work at a level needed for day-to-day life, due to complete or almost complete failure. The most common causes of end-stage kidney disease in the United States are diabetes and high blood pressure. End-stage kidney disease can lead to death if the patient does not undergo dialysis or a kidney transplant.

4. St. John of the Cross's Dark Night of the Soul narrates the journey of the soul from its bodily home to its union with God. It focuses on the painful experiences and spiritual crises that people endure as they seek to grow in spiritual maturity and union with God. St. John of the Cross. Dark Night of the Soul. (Mineola: Dover Publications, Inc., 2003).

5. Daniel J. Levinson. The Seasons of a Man's Life. (New York: Random House Publishing Group, 1978).

6. Sharon Daloz Parks. Big Questions, Worthy Dreams: Mentoring Emerging Adults in their Search for Meaning, Purpose, and Faith. (San Francisco: Jossey-Bass, 2000).

7. An invisible chronic illness cannot be seen by a casual observer. With most illnesses, a person will get sick, but usually he or she will get better. With an invisible chronic illness, this does not happen, since it is ongoing.

8. William Bridges. Transitions: Making Sense of Life's Changes. (Cambridge: DaCapo Press, 2004).

9. Metanoia, which can be translated as "changing one's mind," has both theological and psychological usages. In theological terms, metanoia means to "turn around" by changing a sinful thought or action to gain God's forgiveness. In psychological terms, according to psychiatrist Carl Jung, metanoia is a spontaneous action of the psyche to heal itself of unbearable conflict by "melting down" and then being reborn. The theological meaning of metanoia is how I am using the term.

10. It was only a short journey from Egypt to Canaan by the most direct route. A highway ran up the coast through the country of the Philistines, and the distance was not over 250 miles. It would have taken the Israelites about a month's journey to travel.

CHAPTER EIGHT

The Call of Suffering and Pain
ಌ

Every one of us has suffered a hurt that has robbed us of something much larger than the actual hurt itself. Just as a single pebble can cause an entire pond to ripple, a single painful experience can have far-reaching effects on our lives.

—Rabbi Naomi Levy[1]

But we have this treasure in clay jars, so that it may be made clear that this extraordinary power belongs to God and does not come from us. We are afflicted in every way, but not crushed; perplexed, but not driven to despair; persecuted, but not forsaken; struck down, but not destroyed.

—2 Corinthians 4:7-9

All of us have experienced some type of pain and endured suffering at some point in our lives. But most of us do not equate the painful experiences in our lives with answering a life's calling. In reality, it sounds contradictory to think that when we answer a call, we will experience any suffering and unexpected pain in our lives. Simply put, call-

The Call of Suffering and Pain

ings are not supposed to produce suffering! At least, that is what popular thinking teaches us. During the Q.U.E.S.T._{TM} to discern my own life's calling, I was challenged to look beyond popular thinking about pain and suffering.

After following the call to "face the sun" and learning that I had end-stage kidney disease, I found out that sometimes pain and suffering *are* part of listening to a calling. This became real to me one morning in February, when I awoke to excruciating pain in my big toe on my right foot. Not knowing how I had injured myself, I attempted to do what most men do: I toughed it out by gritting my teeth to bear the brunt of the pain. The pain went away in two days, and all was back to normal until the following February.

As predictable as an Amtrak passenger train leaving the station on time en route to its destination, the pain returned at exactly the same time and in the same toe. And I did the same thing that I did before: I toughed it out. I eventually discovered that the pain that I experienced in my toes was caused by gout[2], one of the many additional health challenges[3] of having end-stage kidney disease.

Sorting through the emotional struggle of coping with end-stage kidney disease that was now coupled with the painful discovery of gout led me to believe that my life had hit rock bottom. I returned to my doctor, seeking answers and secretly needing assurance and comfort. Sensing that I was afraid of what was to come, the doctor reassured me of his care by telling me that he would begin treating my illness with diet, medication, and exercise.

I lost a lot of weight in attempts to halt my kidneys from failing. This provided momentary relief, as my kidneys responded positively to the weight loss. Eventually, however, my kidneys began to continue the slow process of deterioration. My doctor said that eventually my kidneys would shut down, and the only treatment was dialysis or transplant.

When I heard this, I wanted to run home and curl up in a fetal position under the covers. I was terrified of dialysis, and I cried when thinking about having to go to a dialysis center to have my blood cleaned. The news was too much for me to bear. Though unknown to me at the time, this additional diagnosis was like a second call to "face the sun." And as with the initial call, I was just as afraid to listen and follow where the call was summoning me to go.

Fear and Denial

At first I denied that I was sick because I did not feel sick and certainly did not look sick. It took me a long time to come to terms with the doctor's diagnosis. It was hard for me to let go of self-sufficiency, the thought that I was in control of my life.

The old adage that it is "better to deal with the Devil you know than with the Devil that you don't know" describes my feelings of denial. Even though my old way was no longer working for me, I refused to let it go, as it was the only way that I had ever known.

Holding on for Dear Life

A local newspaper interviewed former four-time boxing champion Evander Holyfield before his fight in Moscow. When questioned, the forty-five-year-old Holyfield responded, "People say, 'It's time to do something else other than boxing. It would be easy.'... I say it may be easy for you, but it's complicated to me, because I've never done it. When I'm in the ring, I'm comfortable. When I'm in the gym, I'm comfortable." Holyfield lost that fight. And I was afraid that I would also lose the fight to hold on to my badge of honor of never having suffered from a major illness.

It is hard to try something new after we have been doing things the same way for a long time. Even in the face of overwhelming situations pushing us to move, we continue to hold onto our ropes of security. And when we come to the end of our rope, we try desperately to hold on, hoping that we are rescued before our hands tire. Dangling from the rope like Wile E. Coyote hanging from a cliff in a *Road Runner* cartoon, we hope that the rope does not break.

Clinging to my rope, I did everything that I could possibly do to hold onto the idea that I could be healed. I did not want to undergo dialysis or have a kidney transplant. And I did everything that I could to avoid it. I went to an acupuncturist after hearing a friend say that this practice could help relieve stress and possibly stop the degeneration of my kidneys.

For three months I would lie on a medical exam table to have sterilized needles stuck all over my body in hopes of restoring my health. While this practice helped me to overcome my fear of needles, it did little to help restore the health of my kidneys.

Later I took up Qigong (pronounced "*chee-kung*"), a physical practice that involves bodily movements and breathing. I learned how to relax and how to deal with stress, but my kidneys were still failing.

When Qigong did not work, I began studying Eastern mysticism and the chakra system, as well as Native American and African shamanism, to escape the need for dialysis. In the process, I learned the importance of paying attention to my body. I learned to respect nature and how we are dependent on the earth's resources, but I was still sick.

Finally, I began to analyze my nightly dreams in hopes of being like Joseph: God would provide me with an answer through my dreams. In the process of recording my dreams every morning for six months and then analyzing them, I was able to address some critical emotional issues from childhood that I did know that I had, but I did not receive a dream that portrayed any type of healing for my kidneys.

The Call of Suffering and Pain

Let Go and Let God

During this time of refusing to face the truth about my physical health, I was struggling at sorting through my core assumptions, beliefs, and values about God, myself, and my place in the world that seemed to be coming to an end. Eventually, I realized that it was time to "let go and let God." To put it another way, I had to relinquish my grip on trying to control the outcome of my life and trust that God had my best interests at heart.

Answering the call to "let go" is a conscious decision to abandon our old way of being or relating while remaining open to new qualities about to emerge. Whether this dismantling occurs suddenly or impulsively, or when it is precipitated by unanticipated life crises, such as kidney disease/dialysis, addictive behavior, or a spouse having an affair, we can feel overwhelmed and frightened.

Letting go means allowing life to be the way it is without trying to control or force it to fit our personal script; rather, it entails going with the flow. It is not easy to let go of commitments so tied with our security and self-esteem, and yet to continue in the soul-emptying repetitive tasks of our old lives can make us feel even worse.

At this crossroads we have no choice if we are seeking transformation. It takes strength, courage, wisdom, and sometimes external guidance to survive and thrive during this incredible time of letting go of the past. Once we have let go of the past, we enter a phase of limbo, a time of wandering and healing of our wounded self.

I discovered, much to my surprise, that all of the spiritual lessons that I learned during my Q.U.E.S.T.$_{TM}$ were found in Christianity. Although it took a while to put the pieces together, I was able to see the larger tapestry of the Christian life. What emerged was an understanding of the Christian life as a life of *relationship* and *transformation*—an active relationship with God that transforms life in the present.

Courage under Fire

When I finally gathered the courage to "face the sun" and undergo surgery to prepare my body for dialysis, I was told that I had two options: hemodialysis or peritoneal[4] dialysis (PD). I chose PD so that I would be able to do the procedure myself at home and at work.

The entire process of accepting that I was sick was like Hansel and Gretel's waking up in the forest and discovering that the birds have eaten their breadcrumbs. Tired, confused, and miles away from the comfortable world I had known, I had no idea how to make sense of being "sick" with a life-threatening disease. I was stuck in the mud. The more I tried to get unstuck, the more I kept spinning my wheels and the deeper I sank into the mud.

The Call of Suffering and Pain

Deeper into the Forest

At the deepest darkness of this dark forest season of my life, three persons came forward for testing to be my potential transplant donors. For different reasons, each of the persons was not a possibility for me. Then a fourth person came forward. Things look hopeful, but at the eleventh hour a medical problem was discovered with this potential donor, so in order to avoid further risk to the donor, the process of transplantation was halted. After months of trying to locate a donor, a fifth person, Lesley, came forth.

Lesley and I were colleagues of sorts, both working in higher education and literally connected by the United Methodist Church *connection*[5]. I was the chaplain at United Methodist-related LaGrange College, and Lesley was the administrative assistant and treasurer for the Georgia United Methodist Commission on Higher Education and Campus Ministry, the administrative church body that oversees campus ministry for the state. We were acquaintances through the Commission, seeing each other twice a year at meetings, but more importantly, we were also connected through Lesley's two children, both of whom attended LaGrange—one who graduated and one who transferred from the College.

When Lesley told me about wanting to donate, I nonchalantly dismissed her, not knowing that she had felt that

The Q.U.E.S.T. for Vocation

God was calling her to do this. Lesley contacted Emory University Hospital, where I initially began the kidney transplant evaluation process, and sent her medical history.

Due to a change in my medical insurance coverage, I was no longer eligible to go to Emory for the transplant, so I transferred all of my information to the University of Alabama Hospital in Birmingham, Alabama (UAB). Lesley contacted UAB to schedule an additional pre-screening to be approved as a donor. After undergoing several tests at UAB, Lesley was declared to be a positive match and donor for me.

A Call to Receive Life's Gift

Several months later, I received an e-mail saying, "Merry Christmas." Below this seemingly anonymous greeting were the words, "And call me." It took me a while, but I figured out who had sent me this holiday greeting. It was Lesley. I immediately called her and learned of the gift I was to receive: Lesley's kidney.

When someone asked Lesley why she decided to be my donor, she responded:

> I noticed [about three years ago] at our annual meeting that Quincy had been losing weight. He said he was on a strict diet for health reasons, but he didn't elaborate. The following year he shared with us that he had kidney failure. At that point, I knew I had Quincy's kidney.

Lesley was confident that God had called her to donate her kidney to me. I was not as confident and continued to struggle with the unusual Q.U.E.S.T.$_{TM}$ to answer a mysterious call to "face the sun." Perhaps this said more about my need to hold on to control than anything else.

For some reason, receiving was so much harder than giving was to me. Somehow I had bought into the notion that it was easier to give than to receive. Maybe it was my pride or my fear of being labeled as a taker—taking what I could not afford or what I could not repay, what I desperately needed but saw no way to achieve—that caused me to struggle with accepting the gift of life. But since I was so sick, I quickly swallowed my pride, got past my stubbornness, accepted Lesley's gift, and set a date for the surgery.

Years later, Lesley told me that she was convinced that she received the position at the Commission so that she could give me her kidney. She recalled that she had never heard of the Commission on Higher Education. After a phone interview with the director that she had never met, she took the job without ever visiting the office. She is convinced that her receiving the job was a "God-thing."

The First Transplant

My first transplant occurred on Monday, December 12, 2005. Dionne, my wife, who was my girlfriend at the time,

The Q.U.E.S.T. for Vocation

accompanied me to UAB. As my body was being prepared for insertion of the PD catheter, I was not as nervous or scared as I had been the first time I had surgery. In fact, the doctor commented about my seemingly calm spirit, saying, "You seem to be in good spirits and mighty calm, considering that you are about to have major surgery." I replied, "Sure, I am not worried. My life is not in your hands."

The surgery was successful. I was told that after the kidney had been placed, it began working within five minutes. I experienced minimal pain, and the next day after surgery, I was standing on my feet. The third day after surgery, I was walking around the hospital corridor with my IV pole. By Friday of that week, I was out of the hospital clothes and into my regular clothes. My creatinine (pronounced *kree-at-e-neen*), a waste product of the muscles that is used to measure kidney function, level had fallen to 1.5 mg/dl, which gave me a lot more strength and energy than I had before the transplant when my creatinine was 20 mg/dl.

Even though I had answered the call to "face the sun" and finally passed through the worst of the deep, dark forest, I could not yet put into words that I had completed my Q.U.E.S.T.® All I knew was that I was no longer the same person emotionally, spiritually, or physically. Like the eight-inch surgical incision scar that was etched onto my lower abdomen where my third kidney was housed, my Q.U.E.S.T.$_{TM}$ literally cut away the inconsequential things that had previously consumed my energies.

During the dark forest periods of our lives, we discover a hidden wholeness that rests at the center of the deep, dark forest where God often meets us. When I received the call to "face the sun," I had no idea where my steps would take me and was not expecting to meet God during the process in a new and profound way. Yet, by putting one foot in front of the other, I found what I needed—though at times it was tempered with emotional pain and difficulty.

It was during those painful days that I discovered God's love in a fresh way, which connected me with people and places that transformed my self-image. Along the way, I experienced what writer Joanne Blum calls a "transformative trauma"—a physical, emotional, or psychological crisis that profoundly impacts our lives.[6] These traumatic experiences tell us how we are being shaped and called by life. They also help us to face difficult times, only to be strengthened by relying on inner and external resources that serve as powerful clues to our life's calling.

Questions
1. What is your understanding of pain and suffering, and how does your understanding influence your faith?

The Q.U.E.S.T. for Vocation

2. In the discernment process, everyone takes a number of steps, deliberate or not, to figure out what God is saying. I had to let go and let God during my discernment process, which included struggling with God. Have you ever struggled with God in a similar way?

3. The search to understand what was going on with me physically led me beyond the traditional "pat" answers given by well-meaning Christians and into a dark forest period. Have you ever experienced a deep, dark forest period in your life? What resources helped you emerge from the forest?

Notes

1. Naomi Levy. To Begin Again: The Journey Toward Comfort, Strength, and Faith in Difficult Times. (New York: Ballantine Books, 1998).

2. Gout is caused by a buildup of uric acid. The uric crystals inside the joints cause intense pain whenever the affected area is moved, and gout causes the skin to be swollen, tender, and sore if it is even slightly touched. The reasons for my gout attacks were due to failing kidneys that could no longer flush out the uric acid in my body.

3. As a result of kidney disease, I had also suffered from anemia, a blood disorder caused by iron deficiency, which constantly made me feel weak and tired. Additionally, I suffered from neuropathy, the damaging of the nerves, which coupled with gout, made it nearly impossible at times for me to walk.

4. The kidneys act as a coffee filter by eliminating waste from the body. When the kidneys fail, dialysis is needed

to provide the filtering process. PD is a form of home dialysis in which the patient is taught how to perform the procedure at home. PD does the same work as hemodialysis, which replaces the work of the kidneys. But instead of having blood removed from body to be cleaned as hemodialysis requires, PD uses the peritoneal membrane, the thin tissue that lines the inner wall of the abdomen and covers most of the abdominal organs, to filter waste from the bloodstream that travels across the blood vessels of the peritoneal membrane into a dialysis fluid instilled into the cavity during dialysis. Excess fluids and waste leave the blood and enter a chemical bath solution to remove toxins from the blood.

5. The United Methodist connection is an important part of our denomination's heritage. It is a global network of interactive relationships shared by individuals, local churches, and many other groups in ministry together. Our connection has multiple levels that provide opportunities for service locally and around the world.

6. Joanne Blum. Living Your Calling. (Lincoln: Writers Club Press, 1999).

Chapter Nine

The Call of Curing and Healing
ಬ

We are to learn to listen to the signals of our bodies, honoring them as one of the main ways God speaks to us and by which we can learn much unencountered truth about ourselves and our communities.
—Flora Wuellner[1]

We...groan inwardly while we wait for adoption, the redemption of our bodies. For in hope we were saved. Now hope that is seen is not hope. For who hopes for what is seen?
—Romans 8:23-24

One way to listen to what our lives are calling us to become is to pay attention to the clues that our bodies give us. Our bodies serve as a ceaseless source of information about the state of our internal energies in this space. But too often we ignore the recurrent cues that we get from our bodies in the form of headaches, stomachaches, muscle cramps, and other physical complaints.

If we understood these symptoms as a physical call from God through our bodies, and the depths of beings, then perhaps we would pay attention to the messages that our bodies are trying to communicate to us. Instead of just chalking up our physical discomforts to the "stress" and taking pain medication to give us temporary relief, we can listen to our bodies and thus heed a calling. Body wisdom is a tool we often ignore in discerning a life's calling. We tend to think of discernment as something we do with head and heart alone. But our bodies are gifts from God and can provide a clue to our life's calling and God's will.

We eat too much or too little, or we eat too little during the day and then too much at night. We do not get enough sleep or exercise. It takes a major illness to stop some of us, even when the body has been telling us for years that it is time to stop or slow down or take better care of ourselves. All the while, we may be praying to God for guidance, but we ignore anything that God might be saying to us through our bodies.

When we ignore our bodily symptoms, instead wanting a clearer sign from God—something "spiritual", rather than earthly and physical—an illness gets our attention by disrupting our lives as we knew it.

Body Symptoms as a Calling

Illness can provide an opportunity for us to see our bodily symptoms as a call from our souls. Symptoms are one of the languages that the soul uses to get across to us something about itself. The pain that we experience in our bodies presents to us information that often remains hidden from our awareness until it becomes unbearable.

In many cases, the symptom shows up very early in the process of illness or disease, but we dismiss it or cover it up with pain killers or other activities, or we ignore the symptom altogether. Too often we ignore the recurrent symptoms we get from our bodies. We assume that it is normal to have aches and pains.

When we ignore our bodily symptoms, it is as if we are parents ignoring our child, and our bodily symptom will do everything in its power to call out to us to get our attention. The process with an ignored child goes something like this: the child gently tugs on Mama's leg, trying to get her attention, but is ignored. When this does not work, the child tugs a bit harder. When the child continues to be ignored, then in a last-ditch effort to be heard, she screams at the top of her lungs and acts out to get her mother's attention. Christian writer Parker Palmer illustrates this when he tells a story about ignoring his depression:

> Imagine that from early in my life, a friendly figure, standing a block away, was trying to get my attention by shouting my name, wanting to teach me some hard but healing truths about myself. But I—fearful of what I might hear or arrogantly trying to live without help or simply too busy with my ideas and ego and ethics to bother—ignored the shouts and walked away.
>
> So this figure, still with friendly intent, came closer and shouted more loudly, but I kept walking. Even closer it came, close enough to tap me on the shoulder, but I walked on. Frustrated by my unresponsiveness, the figure threw stones at my back, and then struck me with a stick, still wanting simply to get my attention. But despite the pain, I kept walking away.[2]

All that this friendly figure wanted, Palmer writes, was to get him to turn around and ask, "What do you want?" That is all God wants from most of us, but it is much easier for us to turn our attention to making money, being successful, or clinging to our own sense of who we are rather than paying attention to God.

Our bodily symptoms work in a similar way by using pain as a way to get our attention to tell us that something is wrong. But somewhere in our lives as Christians, we have bought into a false assumption about pain by adopting a worldview that links pain and sickness to sin, which results in dressing our wounds with guilt and judging our illness as a failure of faith. This sort of thinking leads to the assumption that God will heal sickness and alleviate pain only if we put our faith in Him to do so.

Becky's Story

Becky came to college with dreams of playing softball and soccer. One day, while doing conditioning exercises during soccer practice, she started to have pain in her calves that made it difficult to run. Ignoring the pain that was now a daily experience, she continued to push through until she finally realized that she was not going to be able to continue with the season.

She was diagnosed with chronic compartment syndrome in all four compartments in her legs and had surgery later that year. Disappointed at missing her freshman soccer season, she turned her attention to recovering from surgery in time for softball season, which started in the spring. Becky began to wonder why God was allowing this to happen to her. The summer before all her pain began, it had appeared that everything was going according to her plans of being a collegiate athlete.

A few weeks into the softball season, Becky's symptoms returned. She was confused and frustrated. She was sent to several specialists, and after months of pain, anger, and frustration, she was informed that the previous surgery had been unsuccessful. She was re-diagnosed with compartment syndrome in her legs, and she started to question her faith.

The Call of Curing and Healing

After the second round of surgeries was finished, Becky was physically worse than she was before. She spent nearly two years walking on crutches or in a manual wheelchair and no relief was in sight. Nevertheless, she continued praying for God's will to be done in her life, and yet at the same time she began to worry about why her college years were different from what she had expected. She recalls:

> My faith continued to be strained as I became angry at God for letting me be in so much pain. I felt as though I was missing out on so many of the normal college experiences because I physically couldn't participate. I continued to write in my prayer journal, though.

One late night during the spring semester, Becky went to the college chapel to pray. She asked God to take away the pain because she could no longer deal with it. As she prayed, miraculously the pain in her legs disappeared. She was able to walk out of the chapel without her brace or crutches!

Despite her being able to walk with no assistance for nearly four months after her miraculous experience, sadly, Becky's symptoms slowly returned. This time, however, the symptoms and pain were much worse than before. After her symptoms returned, several people who had heard about her chapel "miracle" began to question her, asking why her symptoms had returned if God had really

The Q.U.E.S.T. for Vocation

---

healed her. The assumption was that Becky had lost her faith in God, and this was why her pain returned.

After hearing a lot of different opinions offered by many well-intended persons, and lots of crying sessions in between prayers for healing, Becky finally received an answer to her never-ending physical crisis. She was diagnosed with *paroxysmal exercise-induced dystonia* (PED), an illness of sudden painful, involuntary, and repetitive twisting motions triggered by physical exertion.

A few months later, Becky was able to participate in a chronic pain rehabilitation program at the Mayo Clinic in Jacksonville, Florida. After enduring what she calls the most difficult twenty-one days of her life, she exclaimed,

> I feel as though I have gotten my life back, and I am forever grateful for God for allowing me to endure this journey in order to find my real self. Although I could potentially return to my dream of being a physical therapist, I have changed. I am not the person I was a few years ago. Through my experiences and development, I have deepened my passion for working with children and advocating for them. I am applying to graduate school to become a child life specialist.

At its core, Becky's story is a Q.U.E.S.T.$_{TM}$, in which she had to embrace what her body was attempting to tell her: to let go of her assumptions about God, faith, health, and sickness in order to discover the difference between

The Call of Curing and Healing

healing and curing. When she enrolled in college, Becky had been certain that her life would lead her in the direction of athletics, but an illness in her body called her in a different direction. She had to pay attention to her body as it seemed to be calling her to integrate her physical life into her notion of how God works in the world.

As Becky discovered, we all need to be aware of our body and its symptoms of pain and hurts. How often we hurt—occasionally, once or twice a week, or all the time—as well as when we hurt, can tell us a lot about our proximity to our calling. Powerful signals from our bodies may be disguised as callings to make changes in our lives and reflect on what our souls require.

A Call to Prayer

I recall having an experience similar to Becky's. Shortly after I had been diagnosed with end-stage kidney disease, I received a call of sorts that challenged my assumptions about healing, sickness, pain, and faith. Through a text message inquiring about my availability to attend a college prayer service that one of our student spiritual life groups was conducting, I was invited to come to the chapel at 1:30 p.m. to pray. I agreed to participate.

I arrived at the chapel a few minutes before 1:30 p.m., greeted my students and their campus minister, and took my seat near the back of the chapel. Everyone took a turn to say a prayer out loud. And then it was my turn. I prayed aloud a brief prayer—one that I had being praying silently between the breaks of everyone else's prayer. After the prayer, we all sang "Amazing Grace." I thanked the group and got up to leave.

Before I could get out of my pew to exit the chapel, the campus minister and a couple of students decided that they would have a make-shift "laying on of hands" ritual healing service for my ailing kidneys and to ask God to heal them. I sat in a chair in the middle of the chapel, and everyone hovered over me and began praying. I closed my eyes and felt several hands touch my lower back (in an attempt to find my kidneys), my shoulders, my knee, and my head.

I prayed along with the group, even though I felt more like a hospital patient around whose bed the nurses all crowd, violating the patient's personal space with touching, pricking, pressing, and prodding. In this case, however, the invasive touching, though well-intended, was to gather spiritual information on my failing kidneys and subsequently to ask God to "call down a miraculous healing" and wholeness on my behalf.

Without thinking, I began to act as if somehow this prayer was mysterious and perhaps even magical, guaranteeing that God was to do exactly what was being asked of Him. I was so caught up in the moment that it never occurred to me that prayer, whether it is recited out loud, chanted as a mantra, or simply said in silence, is about letting God in. I would soon learn that prayer provides an open channel for the flow of the Spirit's creative energy, a way of living out what St. Paul the apostle means by "praying without ceasing."[3]

After the service was over, the campus minister was confident that God had heard his and the students' prayer and that my kidneys had been miraculously healed at that moment. Unfortunately, when I went to the doctor for lab work two days later, my blood work gave a report contrary to the hopes of the campus minister: my situation was slowly worsening, and my health was deteriorating.

Since my lab report contradicted the campus minister's report, I had to find another way to make sense of things. Like a professional sports team trailing its opponent and needing to reevaluate its performance, I needed to call a "time-out." I was behind on the scoreboard of life, and there was a need to stop the clock to consider a new strategy and to draw up a new play.

It was not as if I had not already prayed to God about my situation before the healing service. In fact, I had prayed about my failing kidneys every waking moment of the day and often found myself learning to live with the notion that God would answer this prayer with the gift of wholeness and spiritual wellness.

Both Becky and I discovered that there is a subtle but important difference between *healing* and *curing* as understood by most people. Severe, chronic, or terminal illnesses and impairments may not be cured, but in the midst of them, we can be cared for by others and can take care of ourselves to the best of our abilities and by God's grace. Emotional, intellectual, and spiritual wholeness does not require physical wellness.

Healing vs. Curing

Healing is the art of restoring balance, going to the root of the problem, and restoring wholeness to the life of the individual. In Western societies, curing often is used interchangeably with the elimination of symptoms or the disease. Surgery is an example of curing without necessarily healing. The diseased tissue is removed from the body, and the symptoms disappear. Later, the symptoms may reappear in the same place or elsewhere in the body because the imbalance in the individual may be seeking some place to express itself. If balance is not restored, then the cure is only temporary.

The same is true the other way around. A person can be healed and still have the disease. Often the disease has become an entrenched pattern in the body and advances beyond the stage of physical repair. In such cases, people may benefit from emotional relief or a lessening of pain

The Call of Curing and Healing

and suffering. When people are both healed and cured, these cases are called "miracles."

Amid my health ordeals, I focused more on healing my attitude instead of curing my body. Healing my attitude meant coming to terms with knowing that a kidney transplant is not a cure, but simply another form of therapy to treat end-stage kidney disease, which I will always have. And while a transplant is not a cure, it *is* the most effective treatment for kidney failure that we presently have available. Accepting this fact was indeed a miracle of sorts for me, as this type of thinking was far from my limited understanding of healing. In a similar way as Becky's critics believed during her disease relapse, I had been led to believe that when a disease is taken care of through healing or another form of treatment, it is taken care of for good.

Kidney Disease as the Body Calling

In the process of my two-year struggle with nightly dialysis before my first transplant, I had to slowly accept what it meant for my body to revolt on me. It was as if my body was calling me to pay attention to its symptoms of fatigue and fluid retention, as if they were symbols of how I was not listening to my life's calling.

I was unaware of how bodily diseases can help us understand our emotional and psychological struggles through the body's symbolism. This call from my body forced me to ponder the important connections among my body, mind, soul, and spirit. I had to learn how to integrate the forces of pain, doubt, uncertainty, anxiety, fear, denial, sickness, suffering, and surrendering to God into my life.

Eventually, my kidney disease helped me to more fully understand the virtues of compassion, faith, forgiveness, hope, love, and suffering as they relate to the heights and depths of human experience. The kidney disease also led me to an increased interest in the connections between body and soul. And just when I thought that I had responded to the call from kidney disease, I was caught by surprise by yet another summons into the unknown, this time from my newly transplanted kidney.

Questions
1. I introduce the notion that a bodily symptom can serve as a calling. Do you agree with this notion? Is there a possibility that beneath your bodily symptoms there is a calling?

2. There is a popular saying that "Prayer changes things." After my health challenges, my understanding of prayer changed, and now the saying has become "Prayer changes people, and people change things." What is your understanding of prayer?

3. What is your understand of the difference between *healing* and *curing*? Does it matter?

Notes
1. Flora Slosson Wuellner. Prayer and Our Bodies. (Nashville: Upper Room, 1987).

2. Parker Palmer. Let Your Life Speak: Listening to Voice of Vocation. (San Francisco: JosseyBass, 2000).

3. 1 Thessalonians 5:17.

CHAPTER TEN

The Call of Devastating News
ఴ

Obi Wan: *There was nothing you could have done, Luke, had you been there. You'd have been killed, too, and the droids would now be in the hands of the Empire.*

Luke Skywalker: *I want to come with you to Alderaan. There's nothing for me here now. I want to learn the ways of the Force and become a Jedi like my father.*
—*Star Wars: A New Hope*[1]

By the rivers of Babylon—there we sat down and there we wept when we remembered Zion. On the willows there we hung up our harps. For there our captors asked us for songs, and our tormentors asked for mirth, saying, "Sing us one of the songs of Zion!" How could we sing the Lord's song in a foreign land?
—Psalms 137:1-4

The kingdom of Judah's deportation and exile to Babylon by Nebuchadnezzar II in the early sixth century B.C. was one of Israel's most devastating experiences. Compounding the horrific experiences of being

The Call of Devastating News

stripped of their national identity was the fact that Judah had brought about this calamity because of their failure to rid themselves of false gods (idols) and their refusal to listen to prophetic warnings:

> The word of the Lord came to me: Mortal, you are living in the midst of a rebellious house, who have eyes to see but do not see, who have ears to hear but do not hear; for they are a rebellious house. Therefore, mortal, prepare for yourself an exile's baggage, and go into exile by day in their sight; you shall go like an exile from your place to another place in their sight. Perhaps they will understand, though they are a rebellious house.[2]

As the above excerpt from the book of Ezekiel indicates, the captivity in Babylon was presented as judgment, a punishment for the people's idolatry and disobedience of God. My reading of the Bible suggests that the Babylonian captivity was the most devastating news of the Old Testament because it called into question Israel's understanding of God's promise to Abraham and David to be the chosen people, the people with whom God would share an eternal relationship.

In April 2008, nearly three years after a successful kidney transplant, I was blindsided with devastating news that felt similar to Israel's judgment, though I was uncertain why I was being punished. During a routine monthly lab appointment to monitor my transplanted kidney function, I was called by my doctor's assistant and told that I needed to have a test re-administered.

For some reason, my creatinine had risen beyond an acceptable level. When I arrived for my emergency follow-up visit, the doctor would not tell me what level my creatinine had risen, but reading between the lines from his sense of urgency, I knew that whatever the mystery number was, it was not good.

My elevated creatinine level deeply concerned my doctor, and he ordered me to drop everything and rush immediately to UAB for admittance. So with that order from my doctor, I immediately called Dionne and told her the news. Then I went home to pack for both of us to begin the Q.U.E.S.T.$_{TM}$ to UAB.

Emotionally Frozen

During the drive to Birmingham, a lot of scenarios played out in my imagination. "What happens if I lose the kidney?" "Am I ready to undergo dialysis again?" "What if it is an infection?" and "What if it is a blockage?" All of these concerns swam their way to the surface of my imagination.

When we arrived at UAB, we began to look for the Emergency Room (ER). We parked and wandered through a maze, following the signs that finally led us to the ER. At this point I was emotionally numb; it was as if I were in a daydream just walking around on autopilot. I was checked

The Call of Devastating News

into a pod in the triage of the ER. The doctor on call began to ask me several questions. I was asked to strip down and put on a hospital gown. I was hooked up for intravenous therapy and was poked and prodded as if I were cattle on the free range. I eventually learned why my local doctor was so concerned: my creatinine level had skyrocketed from 1.5 mg/dl to 8 mg/dl within a number of days. 8 mg/dl was the same level that I had when I was on dialysis.[3]

The Call of Kidney Rejection

The next morning, after a series of examinations, I was told that my body was rejecting my kidney. It was as if I had received a death sentence from the doctors. I began to cry and wondered why I was experiencing this, as I had done everything in my power to prevent rejection.

A few hours later, as I was still struggling to come to terms with the doctor's diagnosis, the hospital phone rang. I did not feel like speaking to anyone and did not answer it. Then my cell phone began to ring, so I decided to answer. Maurice, a minister friend of mine, was calling to see how things were going. When he inquired about how I was doing, I was honest about my feelings that were not very positive. I went on to tell him that I was in the fog and really did not want to talk about God or faith at the moment. In his efforts to comfort me, he quoted Isaiah 43, saying:

> Do not fear, for I have redeemed you; I have called you by name, you are mine. When you pass through the waters, I will be with you; and when you pass through the rivers, they shall not overwhelm you; when you walk through fire you shall not be burned, and the flame shall not consume you.[4]

Ironically, the scripture had been written to encourage the people of Judah during the Babylon captivity experience—the punishment for the people's action of disobeying God. Maurice meant for the scripture to be a sign of God's *reward* of coming through difficult, life-threatening events without being harmed.

Instead of reward, I experienced the sting of punishment, since at the time I felt the exact opposite of what the scripture was saying. I *was* drowning in the watery chaos of my own emotions, and I *was* being consumed by the fear of what could potentially happen to me. I knew that Maurice was trying to be helpful and pastoral to me, but I could not hear any comfort in his words.

Later the physician's assistant came by and added insult to injury by giving the reason for my kidney rejection: I was rejecting because of the changes in the anti-rejection medication over the past few months while the doctors had been trying to strike a delicate balance of medication in my system. Too much anti-rejection medication would weaken my immune system, potentially causing infection, and not enough medication would cause kidney rejection.

Rejection is what our immune system naturally does to protect itself. The immune system, our body's natural defense, is built into all of the cells in our body and marks the cells in us as "belonging to us." Anything that the immune system finds that does not have these markings (or that has the wrong markings) is definitely "not us" and is therefore fair game. My body saw my transplanted kidney as "not me" and began to reject it. In reality, however, my body was doing exactly what it was designed to do. This is why I interpreted my experience as a punishment, thinking that God was no longer pleased with me and somehow had forgotten that I had answered His call to "face the sun."

Probing for Answers

I was scheduled to have a kidney biopsy—a test in which a needle probes into the kidney to remove sample tissue—to determine why my creatinine levels were so high. It was as if the waste in my body was being stubborn and was not going to cooperate until it received the attention that it needed. The results of the biopsy told the doctors that it was possible to save the kidney from being fully rejected by my body.

In attempts to stop the rejection, my defense system was lowered by heavy doses of steroids. Since this process did not stop the rejection significantly, I was given a more powerful treatment.

The following morning, I received a Peripherally Inserted Central Catheter (PICC) line that has one port for drawing blood and a second port for infusing medication. I was given the first of three six-hour therapy sessions to treat the rejection.

A Crisis of Faith

I was having what Sharon Parks calls a "shipwreck"[5] experience, a crisis of faith that was so disorienting that it was difficult to make sense of things. I thought that I was past suffering. And it was hard to accept that once again, I was no longer in control of my emotions or my body. But most of all, I was scared of what the future would hold for me. To put it bluntly, I did not want to live the story of being a needy and dependant *invalid*: one who is constantly sick and needing to be cared for.

I was literally wiped out, and all I could do was lie in the bed, fading in and out of consciousness. After I was given more treatment, I was told what I already knew from experience—I had picked up an infection. I was growing impatient, and I wanted the entire ordeal to be over and done with.

As they continued to monitor my progress, it was discovered that the PICC line was the cause of the infection.

They removed the PICC line and put in a regular intravenous line to provide access for antibiotics to fight the infection and build back up my immune system. This process tried my patience even more, as it took four people to find a vein without causing me severe pain.

The days of the week began to blur. I was tired. I was hurting. And I was ready for this ordeal to be over. I began to have long talks with God at night. I began to experience a roller coaster of emotions that bounced among anger, fear, sadness and doubt. I began to worry and began asking questions such as "God, where are you?" and "Why is this happening to me again?"

Acceptance and Surrender

After two weeks of testing and therapy, the doctors were satisfied that they had done all that they could medically to halt the rejection. When I arrived for the first biopsy in April, the doctors were optimistic about my creatinine returning to near my post-transplanted level of 1.5 mg/dl. Now, two months into rejection and after a second biopsy, the doctors were not as hopeful and were less sure where my creatinine would finally settle.

Knowing that the doctors were not hopeful was hard for me to accept. It took a lot of patience and praying, but it finally occurred to me that "acceptance" comes when we *surrender:* surrender our need to compare our experiences with those of others as if it were a competition, surrender our self-critical judgments, and surrender our need to completely understand. Surrender is not the same as resignation. Rather, surrendering to the unknown *is* answering a call from God. It is a courageous choice, an act of faith, and trust in God.

Answering the call to surrender challenged my assumptions about God. From my theological education, I knew *about* God, but during this experience, I was being *introduced* to God in a way that suggested that surrendering, suffering, and even failures were somehow part of the entire mystery of God. It was as Christian theologian Paul Tillich once wrote:

> Sometimes at that moment a wave of light breaks into our darkness, and it is as though a voice were saying: "You are accepted. *You are accepted*, accepted by that which is greater than you, and the name of which you do not know."[6]

I knew that I was accepted by God, but I had to learn to accept God's acceptance and surrender my notion of earning God's love and acceptance through my efforts, even if it meant going back to dialysis.

Painful Encounters

On March 9, 2011, nearly two years after my rejection, I went back to peritoneal dialysis (PD) as a daily therapy treatment for my now rejected kidney transplant. I felt like a failure having to return to a world that I had been confident I would never have to revisit as a patient. Returning to dialysis after almost three years of freedom was like taking a step backwards.

I remember thinking that, if somehow this experience was part of God's calling for my life, then I did not want to hear anything else from God at this point. Like the biblical character Job, who questioned God when he lost his health and all his possessions, I began to question God about why I was going through this journey for a second time. Was there some lesson that I had not learned the first time around? Did I need a refresher on some important aspect of life? What was the meaning behind my continued suffering?

The second time around on PD was different. During my first experience, I had never had any complications at all. Unfortunately, a couple of months into the second round of treatment, I began to experience negative numbers on my dialysis machine and "cloudy" PD fluid in my discharge bag, both signs that I was not receiving dialysis as fully as I should.

I called Pam, my PD nurse, to inform her of this new condition. She asked me to bring in a sample from my bag with cloudy PD fluid, and she called me into the dialysis clinic to have my abdomen "flushed" with medicated PD fluid. At the clinic Pam injected an antibiotic into a new PD bag and filled my abdomen with the medicated fluid. The "cloudy" bag was sent to the laboratory for analysis.

After the treatment, I continued PD, despite the potential infection, so that there would not be any interruption of the eliminating waste and fluid from my body. Unfortunately, however, after this initial treatment, I continued to have cloudy bags, and Pam continued the treatments.

In September 2011, during the final night of an administrative cabinet planning retreat in Florida, I had severe pain in my abdomen. Thinking that it was the side effect from all of the seafood that I had eaten earlier that day, and knowing that we would be leaving for home in the morning, I took a Tylenol and went to bed. But I could not sleep, due to the severe pain. I called Pam but did not get an answer. On the six-hour ride home to LaGrange, the pain subsided but did not go away entirely.

The pain worsened that night, and I called to schedule an emergency appointment with Pam for the next morning. Holding my abdomen while slumped over from excruciating pain, I walked in the dialysis clinic's observation room. Pam told me that I needed to have immediate surgery to remove the PD catheter. My greatest fear had come true: I had contracted peritonitis, an infection of the peritoneal membrane, the lining of my abdomen, and I was going to have to do hemodialysis, a procedure that would clean the toxins in my blood, until my peritoneal membrane healed.

After Pam gave me a prescription for pain killers, I discovered that the most common cause of peritonitis is bacterial infection that occurs when bacteria are inadvertently introduced into the peritoneal fluid by improper technique during the connection of the PD bag to the catheter in the abdomen.

Since I had been doing a great deal of traveling during the time that I was getting negative numbers and cloudy bags, Pam determined that my bout with peritonitis was probably caused by the unclean air ducts in the hotel room with a faulty HVAC unit. Though she could not confirm her hypothesis until my lab work came back, her initial diagnosis was based on the cloudy PD drainage after dialysis.

My constant battles with cloudy bags and eventual peritonitis caused the loss of my PD catheter. The catheter was removed, and a temporary access catheter was surgically inserted into my chest through a large vein and secured with a stitch so that I could begin hemodialysis until my peritoneal membrane healed and I could return to PD.

Hemodialysis

I chose to go to the dialysis clinic on Tuesdays, Thursdays, and Saturdays from 6:30 a.m. to 10:00 a.m. for my scheduled dialysis treatments so that I would not miss time at the office. Thinking back several years to when I had initially been told that I would do dialysis and had a brief tour of the dialysis clinic, I began to worry about what my experience would be.

I was weighed on a large scale to get my pre-dialysis weight and assigned a "chair" where the dialysis machine was configured for my treatment. The dialysis technician explained how the machine worked and the process: For three and one-half hours, excess fluid would be removed through large tubes attached to the machine while cleansing my blood of toxins. Afterward, I would be weighed again to get my post-dialysis weight, which would be used as my baseline weight for every treatment going forward.

I was surprised to learn that dialysis can remove only water that is in the blood, and only a small part of the water weight that is gained when the kidneys fail is found in the bloodstream. The technician went on to explain that during a dialysis treatment, pressure from the machine forces fluid in the blood into the dialysis solution and down the drain.

The machine was set to a fluid goal of my "dry weight," or my weight without excess water. Since it was my first hemodialysis treatment, I was unaware that the machine keeps pushing toward this goal, even if there is no more water in the blood. I began to get

The Call of Devastating News

extremely cold, and the machine began to beep very loudly. When the dialysis technician came by to check on my machine, she told me that my blood had become too "dry," making my blood pressure drop and causing me to get really sick.

Apparently too much water had been removed from my blood too quickly, and I became dehydrated. I began to have painful muscle cramps in my legs and got really dizzy. My chair was adjusted so that my head was elevated, and I was given a blanket and pillow to make me feel more comfortable. Now I knew first-hand why so many of the patients that I met on my brief tour of the hemodialysis wing actually dreaded coming to dialysis.

Knowing that I had at least two and possibly three months on hemodialysis, to allow my abdomen to heal so that I could resume peritoneal dialysis at home, I quickly learned about my ideal "dry weight" and brought my own pillow and blanket for comfort. It was hard for me to see how hemodialysis fit into my life's calling. I realized how little I knew or understood God. And like Job, I was hoping that in time that I could say, "I had heard of you by the hearing of the ear, but now my eye sees you."[7] Up to this point, my experience with hearing a life's calling through my body had been a trying one. But nothing had prepared me for the adventure of trying to get rid of the excess water that I would soon encounter.

The Q.U.E.S.T. for Vocation

Questions
1. Having to undergo dialysis for a second time really challenged my faith and my assumptions about God. Have you ever experienced a crisis of faith that challenged your faith? How did you cope during your crisis?

2. One of the hardest things for us to do is to accept that a situation such as an illness is beyond our control and the need to surrender our need to be in control of things and to trust God. What are the areas in your life where you should surrender your need to control the outcome and God?

3. Do you agree with my notion that a painful encounter can serve as a calling from God? If so, have there been any painful encounters that have served as a call from God to change your life's direction?

Notes
1. Star Wars, Episode IV: A New Hope. Dir. George Lucas. Perf. Mark Hamill, Carrie Fisher and Harrison Ford. Lucas Films and 20th Century Fox, 1977. Film.

2. Ezekiel 12:1-3.

3. The kidneys maintain the blood creatinine in a normal range between .8 and 1.3 milligrams per deciliter (mg/dl). An elevated creatinine level signifies impaired kidney function or kidney disease. Abnormally high levels of creatinine thus warn of possible malfunction or failure of the kidneys. When there is a continual creatinine of 10 mg/dl, dialysis is needed.

4. Isaiah 43:2.

5. The metaphor of "shipwreck" can be used to describe times when we experience something unexpected and disappointing. Our world begins to change and perhaps even falls apart. Shipwreck takes several forms, including a family crisis, loss of relationship or identity, and a health crisis. My rejection episode was causing a major health crisis and sent me into a shipwreck experience. The good news is that with every shipwreck experience, there is also the possibility of washing up on a new shore. See Sharon Daloz Parks. *Big Questions, Worthy Dreams: Mentoring Emerging Adults in Their Search for Meaning, Purpose, and Faith.* (San Francisco: Jossey-Bass, 2000).

6. Paul Tillich. "You Are Accepted." The Shaking of the Foundations. (New York: Charles Scribner's Sons, 1948).

7. Job 42:5.

CHAPTER ELEVEN

Missing the Call
ଚ

There is a light in this world, a healing spirit more powerful than any darkness we may encounter. We sometimes lose sight of this force when there is suffering and too much pain. Then suddenly, the spirit will emerge though the lives of ordinary people who hear a call and answer in extraordinary ways.

—Mother Teresa[1]

Jesus said to him, "If you wish to be perfect, go, sell your possessions, and give the money to the poor, and you will have treasure in heaven; then come, follow me." When the young man heard this word, he went away grieving, for he had many possessions.

—Matthew 19:21-22

Jonah is a prophet who refuses God's call.[2] When God calls Jonah to proclaim judgment to Nineveh, the capital of the Assyrian empire, for the people's worship of idol gods and goddesses, Jonah says "no" and attempts to flee. He decides to go in the direction opposite of Nineveh to ancient Joppa, the port city right outside of modern-day

Tel Aviv, to board a ship bound west for Tarshish, a seaport city in Spain.

Once Jonah's ship sets sail on the Mediterranean Sea, God calls up a great storm, and the ship's crew casts Jonah overboard in an attempt to appease God. A great fish sent by God swallows Jonah. For three days and three nights, Jonah languishes inside the large fish's belly. He says a prayer in which he repents for his disobedience and asks God for mercy. God speaks to the fish, which vomits out Jonah safely on dry land.

After his rescue, Jonah obeys the initial call to prophesy against Nineveh; they repent, and God forgives them. Jonah angrily tells God that he knew that God would offer forgiveness if the people turned around. Furious at God's gracious actions towards the Ninevites, Jonah abandons the mission, thinking that God had just spared one of Israel's enemies.

Jonah is not the only person who hesitated a great deal before finally answering God's call. When God calls Moses, he objects to God's call. God says to Moses, "I am sending you to Pharaoh to bring my people the Israelites out of Egypt," and Moses replies, "Who am I to go to Pharaoh...?"[3] Afterward, there is a long conversation between God and Moses, in which God has to reassure Moses several times that He will be with him to help him, but each time Moses finds some new excuse for not answering God's call.

One of the excuses Moses gives God is "But suppose they [the Hebrews] will not believe me or listen to my words, and say to me, 'The LORD has not appeared to you'?"[4] Again God reassures him, but Moses finds another excuse: "Please, my Lord, I have never been eloquent,... for I am slow and hesitant of speech." Again God reassures Moses, and once again Moses makes an excuse: "Please, my Lord, send anyone you decide to send!"[5]

It becomes quite a struggle for God to get Moses to answer His call. Moses knows that it will be difficult to lead the Israelites out of Egypt, and he hesitates many times when called by God, but eventually he answers the call. Like Moses, we often find the process of answering a calling to be difficult, as we do not think that we are capable of fulfilling the task that we are being called to.

Not everybody who is called in the Bible answers God's call. There is the story of the rich young man who turns his back on Jesus' call.[6] According to the story, the young man has kept all the commandments since his youth, and we read that Jesus looks steadily at him and loves him. Jesus asks him to do one more thing: to sell what he has and follow Him. The young man's face falls at the call to sell his possessions and follow Jesus, and he goes away very sad because he cannot let go of his possessions. As in the

Missing the Call

---

case of Moses, the young man is struggling with the twin responses "Yes" and "No."

Answering God's call holds a fascination for him, but it is also frightening. He wants to have everything, but that is impossible. He has to make a choice, but he does not have the ability and lacks the generosity to put Jesus before his possessions. Answering God's call is exciting, but as with every decision we make, it involves saying "no" to other possibilities.

The young man has a vocation, but he chooses not to answer it because he does not want to say "no" to some of the more attractive possibilities that life has offered him. But in saying "no" to his vocation, he surely loses out on greater possibilities and the greater potential for happiness that God's call offers.

From these and several more call stories found throughout the Bible and literature, we find that it takes faith and courage to answer God's call to an unexpected journey. In J.R.R. Tolkien's novel *The Hobbit*, Bilbo Baggins, a young, small hobbit, also discovers that it takes courage to answer the call to an unexpected journey.

An Unexpected Journey

Bilbo, like most hobbits, is comfortable and complacent. He loves the comforts of food, drink, and security. But there is more to Bilbo than his love for comfort and

The Q.U.E.S.T. for Vocation

security. Buried deep within his nature are the makings of a Q.U.E.S.T.$_{TM}$

Bilbo's ancestry is noble by hobbit standards: his father was from the well-to-do, conventional Baggins family, and his mother was from the Took family, the wealthy, eccentric family infamous for their unhobbit-like tendencies to go on adventures. Despite his Took blood, however, Bilbo prefers to stay at home to live a quiet life. All of this changes when the mysterious wizard Gandalf the Grey visits him to invite him to a Q.U.E.S.T.$_{TM}$ for adventure. Initially, Bilbo follows the Baggins' convention for security and politely refuses the request to join the Q.U.E.S.T.$_{TM}$ He responds to Gandalf,

> Sorry! I don't want any adventures, thank you. Not today. Good morning! But please come to tea—anytime you like! Why not tomorrow? Come tomorrow! Good bye![7]

Influenced by the comfort and security of what he has come to know, Bilbo does not heed Gandalf's call. Instead, he tries to ignore Gandalf by sending him on his way. He wants nothing to do with a Q.U.E.S.T.$_{TM}$ as he is convinced that hobbits are not meant to go on adventures.

But Gandalf does not take "no" for an answer. Unbeknownst to Bilbo, Gandalf scratches a secret mark on Bilbo's front door that says, "Burglar wants a good job, plenty of excitement, and reasonable reward." The next

Missing the Call

morning, a dwarf knocks on Bilbo's door. Expecting to see Gandalf at his door, Bilbo is surprised and irritated by the dwarf's presumptuous arrival and his self-invitation to dinner. Shortly afterward, Gandalf arrives with some other dwarves.

Gandalf hatches a plan for Bilbo to accompany the dwarves as a burglar on their journey. The group's Q.U.E.S.T.$_{TM}$ is threefold:

- *Destroy the dragon who seized the mountain from the Dwarves' forefathers;*
- *Recapture the mountain using the secret door; and*
- *Divide the treasure within the hall of the mountain.*

The morning after, Bilbo oversleeps and nearly misses the start of the journey with the dwarves. Along the way, Bilbo discovers that answering the call of a Q.U.E.S.T.$_{IM}$ takes courage.

Missing the Call

Unlike Bilbo, who nearly misses his calling by oversleeping, I actually *missed* the call from the Mayo Clinic for a second kidney transplant on May 8, 2012 at 1:15 a.m. Somehow I had slept through the phone call but was awakened by a mysterious loud bang that shook the house.

When I woke up the next morning and noticed that I had missed the call from the Mayo Clinic, my heart sank. I returned the call and was told that they would call me back within the hour. When Tommy from the Mayo Clinic returned my call, he immediately called me a heavy sleeper. He told me not to worry, as the doctors had determined that the kidney that they had was not the best match for me anyway. He also told me that he would be calling back soon, since I was now near the top of the list to be transplanted from a deceased donor.

I could not believe that I missed the call that I had been waiting for almost two years ago to receive. It became very hard for me not to play the blame game and beat myself up with negative and condescending thoughts, such as

> How stupid can you be, Q? Are you incompetent? You missed the call, and there is no telling when or if the call will ever return. How are you going to tell people that you slept through your life-line call?

The onslaught of negative feelings became too much to bear, so I decided not to think about it any further. But I knew that at some point, I would have to deal with these feelings. I was hoping that I would get a return call before I was forced to deal with those feelings of stupidity and incompetence.

Missing the Call

Still hearing the knock that occurred after the big bang that woke me the previous night, I decided to go down into the basement to investigate. One-third of the basement had flooded with about eight inches of water. I thought that perhaps it was a good thing that I missed the call, since the kidney was not a good match anyway. Like the young rich man who makes the difficult choice of not following Jesus, I was faced with making a difficult choice: Go to Jacksonville to get a new kidney, or fix the leak in the basement. Although the choice was made for me by the kidney not being a match, I was still worried as to whether or not I would be ready when or if the call returned.

The Call Returns

After church, a couple of months later on Sunday, July 1, Dionne and I went out to lunch at LongHorn Steakhouse with David, the provost of the college, and his wife, Donna. Right after I received my salad, my cell phone began to vibrate. I pulled it from my holster and saw that it was Tommy from the Mayo Clinic calling again. I answered with baited breath as Tommy said: "Mr. Brown, I'm calling from the Mayo Clinic with a kidney with your name on it."

Immediately, Dionne and I left LongHorn to drive home and pack. On the way, I called Delta Airlines to make emergency travel arrangements, since we had to be in Jacksonville, Florida, no later than 9:00 p.m. that night.

It was a six-and-one-half-hour drive from our house to Jacksonville, and we had not packed!

As we were driving to the airport, I recalled how I had missed the first phone call, and then all of the negative feelings from missing the call and memories from my first rejection episode came flooding back. Fighting back tears of anguish, I attempted to allow the images and feelings to display themselves in my mind's eye. And much like the words that had called to me during my encounter with the red-tailed hawk several years earlier, once again, *The Voice* began to speak, saying:

> Tears will flow when you're on the other side again. It's a long time coming, but you will finally feel like your soul's self again. Another kidney transplant and you will be "planted in soul" once more. We all start with two natives, the third was rejected, and now one more will give you four.

I felt as if I was being comforted by a voice that was similar to that of Kick-Kick, my childhood pillow, whose words were like the oracle at Delphi,[8] giving me a prophetic prediction for my future. I had finally received the "reward" of coming through the emotional "waters" and "fire" of fear that I had needed to experience so badly when Maurice called me during kidney rejection at UAB.

Missing the Call

Having received the prediction, I became anxious and wanted to get to the Mayo Clinic as quickly as possible. When we arrived at the airport, all I could think of was making it to the plane on time. Boarding the plane, I was finally able to breathe a sigh of relief, knowing that I was en route to the Mayo Clinic.

We arrived at the ER for admission at 7:04 p.m., and I was assigned to Room 319 at 8:30 p.m. After several preparatory tests and blood samples, I was called at 2:50 a.m. to go to surgery. The transplant surgery took three hours, and I was brought back to Room 319. I was told that my creatinine before the transplant had been 22.6 mg/dl, and after the new kidney was transplanted, it dropped immediately to 20.2 mg/dl. Within a couple of weeks, it finally settled to the normal functioning level of 1.3 mg/dl.

Thirty-seven days later, I was allowed to return home with a new kidney. It was a five-week journey of listening to soul and vocation and finding wholeness that began with a whirling event of receiving the phone call from the Mayo Clinic while having lunch. It was hard to wrap my mind around the entire event. And it was even more overwhelming to have so many people make such a fuss about me.

Being a kidney transplant patient for the second time around was an extremely humbling experience. In fact, some have even called this experience a miracle. And while I can certainly understand their perspective, I do not know if I would call it a miracle *per se*, but it was definitely a long awaited "God-thing" for me, in which I had to learn and relearn that faith is a life-long spiritual practice. Faith required me to let go of control and trust the *Infinite Mystery of Presence*, the new understanding of God that I came away with from answering the call to embark on a Q.U.E.S.T. for health and wholeness. And I was awestruck to enter into a new and profound way of the Christian mystery of someone having to die in order for me to live.

After the transplant, I felt better physically than I had in a long time. I was very happy that I was no longer dependent upon a machine for life. But my delight in a new-found freedom from dialysis was mixed with a bit of guilt from profiting by someone else's loss. The thought that some other family had lost a loved one and had been altruistic enough to donate their organs was overwhelming. Surprisingly, it made the Christian story of crucifixion and resurrection more personal and accessible to me. It was a personal *Good Friday* moment, the day when we remember and celebrate the death of Jesus on the cross and what it accomplished for humanity.

After my transplant, I thought a lot about the phrase "Christ died for our sins." Before the second transplant, I had frequently preached about it on Sunday mornings from the pulpit. Now, I had had an experience that caused me to further investigate the phrase. When I think about how people typically used this phrase, it feels more like our sinfulness *caused* Jesus to be killed and his dying *caused* God to love us. Paradoxically, this perspective leaves us feeling guilty and not necessarily grateful, empowered, or transformed, as we are taught that we are supposed to feel. Perhaps this was why I felt guilty after receiving my second transplant in seven years.

Answering the Call

During my first transplant, I had a living donor kidney. My second kidney transplant came from a cadaver donor whom I did not know. Because of the gift from an unknown giver, my entire world had been changed. When I answered the call to face the sun, I had no idea that the redemption process of "at-one-ment" requires that we participate in receiving.

Put another way, my second transplant provided "at-one-ment," a physical, spiritual, and psychological transformation that helped me to understand whom I was called to be in God's plans: one who uses his own experiences of suffering to help dialysis and kidney transplant patients who struggle to answer the painful call of "facing the sun" of fear, doubt, and uncertainty. I felt compelled to answer a call to live my life in honor of my unknown but

The Q.U.E.S.T. for Vocation

yet connected donor, since I had a piece of his or her organ inside of me, helping me to live.

Questions
1. Jonah's story is instructive regarding a refusal of God's call. Has there ever been a time in your life when you refused to answer God's call? What was the result of your refusal?

2. When God calls us, He often calls more than once. The call will always return. In the Bible, God often called people's names twice. In my encounter, the transplant call came twice. Why do you think that God calls us more than once?

3. I mention that I had to relearn that faith is not only a relationship in seeking understanding, but it is also a life-long spiritual practice of letting go of control and trusting the Infinite Mystery of Presence. How might you engage in the practice of letting go of control and trusting the Infinite Mystery of Presence?

Notes
1. Quoted by Kirsti A. Dyer, "9-11: United in Courage and Grief," www.journeyofhearts.org/kirstimd/911_story.htm.

2. Jonah 1:1-3.

3. Exodus 3:1-11.

4. Exodus 4:1.

Missing the Call

---

5. Exodus 4:10-13.

6. Mark 10:17-22.

7. J.R.R. Tolkien. The Hobbit, Or There and Back Again. (London: George Allen & Unwin, 1937).

8. The word oracle comes from the Latin word "to speak," and refers to a priest making a prophetic prediction. In ancient Greece, the site of the Delphic oracle was where pilgrims would come from all over the ancient world to receive a prophetic prediction.

PART THREE

The Call of the Soul

☙

CHAPTER TWELVE

The Call of Imagination and Soul

ಐ

"Work in the invisible world at least as hard as you do in the visible."
—Rumi[1]

"Take my yoke upon you, and learn from me; for I am gentle and humble in heart, and you will find rest for your souls."
—Matthew 11:29

I am interested in using the imagination to see the "invisible" and the spiritual at work in our lives. This interest leads me to the mysteries of life that surround us inwardly and outwardly. "Providence" is the name that theologians give to this concept, and it is understood as a divine plan.

Using the imagination as a framework to interpret a life's calling, I believe that God speaks to us in a variety of ways, including, but not limited to, a phenomenal experience with God without words. The result is an overwhelming message or strong impression, a vision that requires additional reflective and prayerful interpretation, nightly dreams, intuition, and the imagination, the production of inner picture-images or symbols that flash across the inner screen of our mind. The many ways in which God speaks to our hearts and souls suggest that there is in God some intentionality, some orientation or direction, some purpose or plan that invites us in and moves us forward.

Our callings often are expressed through the images that arise in the imagination. It is therefore necessary to become aware of this deep imagination in which the images and impulses of your deepest self appear. Similar to a perspective of archetypal psychologist James Hillman, I believe that the imagination is one of the primary activities of the soul. Starting with the Jungian notion that "image is soul[2]," Hillman suggests that soul is understood to be the source of images—dreams, stories, fantasy, and the poetic response.

Living our calling is primarily a prayerful and intuitive process. It requires us to pay attention to our souls to see divine synchronicities[3] that uncover our core stories. Often these divine synchronicities that hint at our core stories catch our attention in such a way that we intuitively understand we are following the right track or on the wrong track. They may show up as God's way of offering reassurance that everything is going to be okay. Other times, like a call

The Call of Imagination and Soul

to follow along the yellow-brick road to the Emerald City in Oz, they occur to tell us that there is something more to come and that we should head off into a new direction, as a young administrator quickly discovers.

The Land of Oz

Daphne works as a senior level administrator in a national non-profit organization. Much of her energy is spent in developing leadership development strategies and programs, networking with future partners, providing administrative oversight, and consulting for regional volunteers. While she is good at her job, she has begun to sense that there is something else that she needs to be doing, but she is not quite sure what that something is. She is trying to determine what her next professional move should be. During her discernment to follow the hunch that she believes is calling her to another place, doubts and fears begin lurking in the background of her mind about taking the risk to leave what is known.

I met with Daphne in an attempt to help her with making sense out of her hunch about needing to make a professional change. I discovered that since her childhood, the film *The Wizard of Oz*[4] has held a fascination for her. She comments,

Even as a child I had a sense of wonder, to follow Dorothy's journey from a "black and white," boring life to find unexpected companions with strength that she couldn't have imagined back in Kansas. I saw this as a movement from the "black and white," two-dimensional world into a three-dimensional world full of color and opportunities. Following the yellow-brick road begins as a dance, but it soon becomes a perilous journey of epic proportions.

We continued to discuss how *The Wizard of Oz*, the film adapted from L. Frank Baum's book *The Wonderful Wizard of Oz*[5], tells the story of Dorothy Gale, an orphan, who takes a leap of faith and goes through various disasters in her journey. Daphne watched *The Wizard of Oz* throughout her childhood and vividly remembered the "Surrender, Dorothy" scene from the film. In this scene, the Wicked Witch of the West appears in the sky, riding her broomstick and skywriting the words "SURRENDER, DOROTHY" in an attempt to convince Dorothy and her companions to abandon their Q.U.E.S.T.$_{TM}$ This dramatic scene burned itself in Daphne's imagination, as she recalled:

> Since I first started watching that movie every year as a child, that scene sticks with me. I would always think, "No Dorothy, don't give up. You have to keep going on the yellow-brick road!" The first time I saw it, of course, I didn't know what was at the end of the road, but I wanted to believe it was good. With later viewings

> I just wanted her to know that her journey wouldn't turn out the way she expected—but still good.

I hinted to Daphne that she should pay closer attention to the story and view it as a template to help her to discern what was next for her, since it sounded as if she had identified so strongly with Dorothy's experience. In particular, I asked Daphne to discern what it meant for her when Dorothy finally makes it to the Wizard but discovers that he is a fraud and does not have the answers that she is seeking. Her response alluded to knowing that, although the answers Dorothy has been seeking have actually been within Dorothy's grasp all of the time (represented by her ruby slippers, which, when clicked three times, provide her with a way back home), she has to take the Q.U.E.S.T.$_{TM}$ in order to embrace her own strength.

I determined that Daphne had been intuitively attracted to Dorothy's story of *The Wizard of Oz* since like Dorothy, she, too, had been called to a Q.U.E.S.T.$_{TM}$ for "home." This meant that Daphne would need to feel at home with "Kansas," which represented a metaphor for all of the parts of her work life that were similar to the mundane chores of the "black and white" farm scenes from the film. At the same time, she would also need to embrace the "Oz" part of herself, the metaphor for a bountiful land of brilliant colors and possibilities, that seemed to be calling her to "somewhere over the rainbow" where birds fly freely and clouds are far behind her.

Her need for a professional change was an "Oz-like" calling to take a leap of faith and travel the yellow-brick road. This would require a Q.U.E.S.T.$_{TM}$ to move her from beyond being what she called "a dependent people-pleaser" to becoming a person of courage to pioneer a new trail for home. In her struggle to consider answering this calling, she hinted at the tug of war of her internal dueling natures represented by "Kansas" and "Oz." She stated:

> I feel that in my current position, I'm being exposed by the spelling out in the sky "Surrender," and everybody sees it. I keep telling myself "You got to stay on the journey. There's got to be something better." I'm not turning back, I've put all my energy into my career, and turning back is not an option. People will tell you to surrender. The temptation comes from surprising places: people who have said that I have reached the top. Assessment from others that where I am is the apex is a way of saying "Surrender further dreams." The journey continues and evolves.

As I and many others like Daphne have discovered, when considering a life's calling, at some point, we will come face to face with the need to use the *imagination* to help us to navigate the Q.U.E.S.T.$_{TM}$ that beckons us to follow. Imagination incorporates the ability to comprehend, manipulate, deconstruct, and reconstruct symbols, in order to make sense of emerging new images. For Daphne this means using her imagination to construct new meaning out her experiences by using Dorothy's Q.U.E.S.T.$_{TM}$ in Oz as a template to help Daphne to find a new sense of "home" in her professional life.

Daphne learned from her interaction with *The Wizard of Oz*, that imagination literally means "to shape into one," and includes the ability to form images and sensations when they are not perceived through sight, hearing, or other senses.[6] Imagination helps us to provide meaning to our life experiences. Put another way, imagination serves as "the eye" of the soul:

> Imagination is the chief highway to the heart of [humanity]. We often speak of the avenues to the soul, and refer to the eye gate and the ear gate. However, every avenue which we employ must lead on to the main highway to the heart, and that highway is imagination. We may use beautiful pictures to attract attention, to appeal to the eye. Why? Because through the eye the imagination is captured. It seems to be psychologically true that what gets your attention gets you![7]

What is Soul?

I have been called an "old soul." Most of the time, I have taken this as a compliment, depending on whether or not the emphasis is placed on "old" or "soul." Part of

The Q.U.E.S.T. for Vocation

this designation probably comes from listening to soul music[8] at an early age. Surrounded by thirteen first cousins who were at least ten to fifteen years older than me, I was heavily influenced by the music that they listened to. The most prominent music genre that I heard during those early years was *soul*, the gospel-style of music that featured secular lyrics.

Listening to the lyrics from artists such as James Brown, Otis Redding, Aretha Franklin, Isaac Hayes, Gladys Knight, Curtis Mayfield, Patti LaBelle, the Stylistics, the Temptations, Marvin Gaye, and the Commodores taught me what it meant to be soulful. Soul music captured my imagination and stirred my soul by highlighting the themes of triumph, suffering, love, and hope in its songs.

In his book, *Care for the Soul*, spiritual writer Thomas Moore writes that "soul is not a thing, but a quality or dimension of experiencing life and ourselves."[9] It has to do with imagination and depth, value, relationships, and the seat of our emotional lives. According to the Genesis account, God created human beings. God breathed life into the unanimated humans, and we became living souls:

> Then God said, "Let us make humankind in our image, according to our likeness; and let them have dominion over the fish of the sea, and over the birds of the air, and over the cattle, and over all the wild animals of the earth, and over every creeping thing that creeps upon

the earth." So God created humankind in his image, in the image of God he created them; male and female he created them.

...then the LORD God formed man from the dust of the ground, and breathed into his nostrils the breath of life; and the man became a living soul.[10]

Throughout history there have been many attempts to answer the question "What is the soul?" The Greek philosopher Plato believed that the soul was immortal and that there was life after death, following the separation of the soul from the body. Plato's student Aristotle thought that all living things had souls, and a creature's *soul* was its "principle of life"—that which distinguished it from a corpse or other inanimate thing. According to Aristotle's line of thinking, the distinctive thing about humans, however, is that as well as having a soul, we are also capable of rational thought.

In recent years, psychology—the discipline that literally means "the study of the soul"—has added to the definition of *soul*. Sigmund Freud, the father of psychoanalysis, posits that the soul is composed of three parts.[11] Following along a similar path as Freud's protégé Carl Jung, psychologist James Hillman outlines in his book *The Soul's Code: In Search of Character and Calling*[12] what he calls the "acorn theory" of the soul. His theory suggests that each of us holds the potential for the unique possibilities inside ourselves, just as an acorn holds the pattern for an oak tree. Hillman goes on to say that the unique and individual energy of our souls is contained within and displayed throughout our lives, which is often shown in our calling and life's work.

Imagination is also the creative activity of listening to the soul, the essence of our being that affects our thinking and feeling, our intuiting, and our sensing. It expresses our spiritual life, which speaks first in images before it speaks in words. Imagination serves the soul as our bridge back into the space we entered so effortlessly as children when we began to play.

For many people, however, talking about the soul is extremely uncomfortable. But what is *soul*, and why does the idea of talking about it in public make us so uncomfortable? For many of us, we have been taught that our soul is a private matter and must not be discussed in public. In fact, words such as *soul, passion, zest, faith, spirit,* and *heart* are not welcomed in much of our public discourse.

Between Head and Heart

It is not possible to look on a medical X-ray and locate the soul in the same way that we can locate the kidneys. This is because the soul is without physical form. Since it is the essence of who we are as human beings, the soul

The Call of Imagination and Soul

resides between "head" and "heart" and is ultimately the place of imagination.

When thinking about how my physical experiences of kidney disease might relate to soul, I have come to see my experiences as a symptom of "loss of soul." When soul is neglected, it does not just go away; the signs of neglect appear symptomatically in obsessions, restlessness, anxiety, addictions, disease, violence, and a loss of meaning.

Throughout my Q.U.E.S.T.$_{TM}$ to follow a call towards health and wholeness, I have learned, in large part thanks to my kidney disease, to pay attention to images, which always lead to feelings. The feelings that emerge from the images provoke interpretations, which finally affect an application to our daily lives. Since the soul loves to imagine, I have started to pay attention to images. In particular, I have learned to pay attention to the images of soulfulness: good food, good music, satisfying conversation, and genuine friends.

Soul, as I discovered, is found in attachment, love, and compassion. The soul listens to metaphor, stories, poetic expression, and music. The soul is moved by emotion-laden expressions. Recognizing this, I decided to use my crisis of kidney failure as an opportunity for spiritual growth and personal transformation. But most importantly, my kidney disease helped to strengthen my religious faith in God's grace that forced me to come to terms with knowing that I was in need of healing my physical body and my soul.

The Matrix

In the 1999 science fiction adventure film *The Matrix*[13], Thomas Anderson embarks on a Q.U.E.S.T.$_{TM}$ to answer a question that torments his soul. Anderson works as a computer programmer at a software company. But at night, he takes on an alias and becomes the freelance computer hacker known as "Neo."

There is a deep emptiness troubling Neo, and he cannot put his finger on it until he meets Trinity, another computer programmer and hacker, at a night club. Trinity whispers to him, intuitively sensing his question: "I know why you're here, Neo….It's the question that drives us. It's the question that brought you here. You know the question, just as I did." Neo responds, "What is the Matrix?" Trinity replies, "The answer is out there, Neo. It's looking for you. And it will find you if you want it to." Apparently the question of the Matrix has been gnawing at Neo his entire life, yet he has never put it into words before now.

Neo accepts this mysterious calling and discovers that the Matrix is a sophisticated computer program that has imprisoned most of the human race. Morpheus, a legendary computer hacker who has been on the run from police forces around the world, explains to Neo that the

Matrix is everything he sees around him, but the world that Neo has assumed to be real is actually a computer-generated dream. And Morpheus believes that Neo is "The One" who will change the shape of the Matrix according to his own will in order to work within the program and free humanity.

A Soulful Journey

As Neo discovers in his Q.U.E.S.T.$_{TM}$ to control the Matrix, which requires him to answer the call of his troubled soul, nothing is more important to discerning a calling than the need to tend to our soul—that is, our inner life. Tending to our inner lives builds our receptivity to internal and external guidance in the same way that a regular fitness program builds muscles. The "spiritual muscle" we work on building comes from intuition and the openness that is achieved through prayer.

Whether we recite a prayer aloud, chant a mantra, reflect on a scripture or biblical image, or simply sit in silence, the important thing is that we do pray—routinely and authentically, so that we let God in our lives and learn to attune ourselves to God. Jungian analyst and pastoral counselor Jerry Wright describes his life's calling as a soulful journey that has opened him up to Mystery. He writes:

> The more I try to understand about my life and the life of our world, the less certain I am about how it all will work out, and yet the more confident I am that my little span of life, against the backdrop of eternity and timelessness, is important, and that my minute role in the great drama of life is meaningful, that it is accomplishing something. I get glimpses of that. We are birthed by a mystery. We are moved by mysterious forces and fate throughout our lives. And we are always moving toward a mystery which is our end, or maybe our beginning. In more traditional language, we have come from God and we are going to God, and while we live we belong to God. Thanks be to God.[14]

Looking back on my journey via kidney disease through the lens of a life's calling, I recognize that the journey was both physical and soulful. It literally threw together my body and imagination, forcing me to live in the tension between them by watching the images and experiencing the feelings that emerged from this tension.

From this mystery, I have learned that with a symbol, there is no stopping point, no end to reflection, no single meaning, and no clear signal what to do next. In other words, there was no thesaurus of body imagery available to me; I had to trust God. Consequently, my healing was less a work to remove pain, and more about stimulating my imagination to receive grace from God, so that I could reflect more deeply about what God desires for my body and life.

I also recognize that it would have been helpful for me to use my imagination to interview my kidneys well before dialysis by asking: Are you relaxed? Are you enjoying your activity of balancing water? Or am I doing something that is making you depressed? While some may find such conversation frivolous, I am serious when I suggest a ritual exercise such as this that taps into the body and imagination. I suggest this since the word *disease* means "not having your elbows in a relaxed position." When we look at this symbolically, *disease* may mean having no elbow room, being cramped with a loss of freedom and pleasure.

Could it be that my kidney disease was my body and soul talking to me about having "no elbow room," and experiencing a loss of pleasure? If so, then perhaps the meaning behind my kidney disease had to do with my relearning to trust God and enjoy life, finding pleasure in the moment, accepting and making the most of relationships. Of course, I suggest this since the kidney is the organ that regulates water in the body. Water, traditionally, is known as a symbol of the emotions and the world of feelings and pleasure, as well as a cleansing agent and the renewal of life. Perhaps through kidney disease, God was offering me an option.

I have come to believe that this was the message that my body was sending me. Put another way, my kidney disease, dialysis, and transplant were the initiatory phases on my journey that forced me to explore the inner life of compassion. I am reminded of Jesus' story about God's compassionate nature.

In Aramaic, the word for "compassionate" literally translates as "wombishness," the capacity to be warm, life giving, nurturing, inviting and tender. Therefore, I now see that the objective of my journey into the deep, dark forest was about compassionate love: learning to serve, learn, and teach as many people as possible the lessons of compassion and love.

In many ways, my experience was a journey of love to bring my imagination into a relationship with my body—a kind of incarnation. As I have discovered, when bringing imagination to the body, we cannot expect dictionary-type explanations and clear solutions to problems. Much like that of St. Paul the Apostle, my journey initiated me into an experience of God's hidden wisdom in a mystery, which God predestined before the ages for our glory. In my case, this mystery was a journey of love—the intersection of heaven and earth, the visible and invisible, imagination and body, reason and relationship, head and heart, and spirit and soul.

The Call of Imagination and Soul

Through several reflections on my experiences, I used my imagination to place myself in the biblical stories of struggle and illness—such as Jacob's struggle with the angel at the Jabbok River[15] while he is en route to meet with his brother, from whom he has stolen the family's coveted birth right, and the woman who touches Jesus' garment in hopes of being healed from her infirmity that she has suffered with for twelve years[16]—I was able to listen to God's voice of comfort, which made my experiences bearable. Little did I know that in inserting myself into these stories to discover a life's calling, I was following an ancient Christian practice called *contemplation* that was part of Ignatian spirituality.[17]

Imagination as Spiritual Exercise

Ignatius of Loyola was a Spanish theologian who founded the Society of Jesus, the Christian religious order of the Roman Catholic Church that would be later called the Jesuits. Ignatius was convinced that God speaks to us through our imagination, thoughts, and memories.

During his personal experience of seeking to be "at one" with God and to discern God's will, Ignatius kept a journal that chronicled his spiritual insights and experiences. He later added to his notes as he directed other people in the journaling exercises and discovered what *worked* and what did not. Eventually Ignatius gathered all of his prayers,

The Q.U.E.S.T. for Vocation

meditations, reflections, and directions into a carefully designed framework of a retreat, which he called "spiritual exercises." One of the key exercises for Ignatius was what he called "contemplation," which emphasizes a person's relying on his or her imagination to place him- or herself in a setting from a biblical story.

From my experiences with contemplation, I discovered that imagination and soul both use images to convey through their shapes, form, and emotional authority a power of reality that lies at the heart of things, that *connects* the visible world to the invisible world. In a real sense, the principle use of imagination is to inform and vitalize human life in the visible world. It is to create life itself, certainly to create human communities, probably to create all of the informed gestures of love that we know.

Whether we know it or not, many of our religious activities depend on the imagination to foster devotion to nourish our souls. Many of us know how to be busy, but we may not know how to be still. While we may be acquainted with the notion of God in heaven, we are complete strangers to Emmanuel, the God who lives with us. We focus on the wrong places. We are facing the wrong direction, as I learned from my encounter with the red-tailed hawk and had to turn about to "face the sun." Instead of looking upward and towards the outside for answers, we need to look inward and downward into our souls. Life's deepest lessons are found often where we least expect them: the soul, where there is always a constant flow of images to discern.

Constant Flow of Images

The activity of the soul consists of the constant flow of images that move through dreams, daydreams, fantasy, and stories. Soul can be experienced as the dimension of imagination that frames our experiences with meaning to determine how we see the world around us. Soul is a quality of experiencing life that has to do with depth, value, relationships, heart, and personal substance. Soul has to do with authenticity—the connection between heart and mind, mind and emotion, and darkness and light. To serve the imagination is to serve the soul, which is essential in the process of achieving wholeness—the attitude that goes beyond mutually exclusive opposites and strives for an integration of these opposites.

My journey into the deep, dark forest forced me to let go of reason and my sense of control and security. This was the equivalent of an emotional death. I was feeling lifeless, floating in tumultuous waters downhill, around sharp curves and finally coming to halt, no longer the same within. But although I have passed through the waters, by the grace of God, I was not overwhelmed by them. I praise God, for God is good all the time.

The Q.U.E.S.T. for Vocation

Questions
1. What is your understanding of soul?

2. Have you ever considered God speaking to you through your imagination, dreams, and other experiences?

3. My journey through kidney disease was a life's calling that was both physical and soulful, as it literally threw together my body and imagination, forcing me to live in the tension between them. Have you had an experience that forced you consider the importance of your body and your soul?

Notes
1. Mawla Jalladdin Rumi. "Work in the Invisible." Mathnawi Rumi Translation of Books III and IV. Vol. III. (Gibb Memorial Trust, 1930, reprinted 1991).

2. Carl Jung. The Collected Works. Volume 13. Translated by R.C.F. Hull. (Princeton: Princeton University Press, 1953).

3. I have always heard the phrase, "God works in mysterious ways, His wonders to perform," a paraphrase of the hymn "God Moves in a Mysterious Way" by William Cowper. "Divine synchronicity" suggests that the seeming coincidences in our lives are actually divine interventions as described in Cowper's hymn and experienced as "ah-ha" moments, providing opportunities to trust how our lives unfold.

4. The Wizard of Oz. Dir. Victor Fleming. Perf. Judy Garland, Ray Bolger, Jack Haley, Bert Lahr, and Frank Morgan. Metro-Goldwyn-Mayer, 1939. Film.

5. L. Frank Baum. The Wonderful Wizard of Oz. (Chicago: George M. Hill Company, 1900).

6. For many Romantic writers, including Samuel Taylor Coleridge and John Keats, imagination is creation. Coleridge says that imagination is "the living power and prime agent of all human perception, and is a repetition in the finite mind of the eternal act of creation in the infinite I am." According to this statement ,the human imagination, at its highest level, inherits and maintains the divine creative endeavors of the "Great I Am" of the Old Testament. Samuel Taylor Coleridge. Biographia Literaria: The Collective Works of Samuel Taylor Coleridge, edited by James Engell and W. Jackson Bate, (Princeton: Princeton University Press, 1983).

7. Adlai A. Estab. "The Larger Outlook: Imagination—Highway to the Soul." 14 Nov. 2012. <http://www.ministrymagazine.org/archive/1950/September/imagination-highway-to-the-soul>.

8. Soul music made its way north, east, and west via the same train routes that carried rural Black workers from their homes in the South to the industrial North. Migrating to the North, the music of these "blues people" fused with the sophisticated urban sounds of jazz to create the sound first called "race music" and then later referred to as "rhythm & blues" (R&B). As R&B began to gain acceptance among whites, it became split artificially and was known as "rock 'n' roll" (for Whites only) and "soul" (for Blacks only). Eileen Southern. The Music of Black Americans, Third Edition. (New York: W.W. Norton & Company, Inc., 1997).

9. Thomas Moore. Care of the Soul: A Guide for Cultivating Depth and Sacredness in Everyday Life. (HarperCollins Press: New York, 1992).

10. Genesis 1:26-27; 2:7.

11. Sigmund Freud's theory of the soul or psyche suggests three categories: a) the id, which represents the instinctual drives of an individual and remains largely unconscious; b) the super-ego, which represents a person's conscience and internalization of societal norms and morality; c) the ego, which is conscious and serves to integrate the drives of the id with the prohibitions of the super-ego. Freud believed this conflict to be at the heart of mental disorders.

12. James Hillman. The Soul's Code: In Search of Character and Calling. (Warner Books Edition: New York, 1996).

13. The Matrix. Dir. Larry and Andy Wachowski. Perf. Keanu Reeves, Laurence Fishburne, and Carrie-Anne Moss. Warner Bros. Pictures, 1999. Film.

14. Jerry R. Wright. "The Image and the Mystery." The Rose: Inviting Wisdom in our Churches. Winter-Spring 2009 Issue 15.

15. Genesis 32:1-31.

16. Mark 5:21-34.

17. St. Ignatius of Loyola, Trans. by Anthony Mottola. The Spiritual Exercises of St. Ignatius. (Garden City: Doubleday. 1964).

CHAPTER THIRTEEN

The Call of the Music Within
〜

What God wants for us and from us has something central to do with what we most deeply and truly want for ourselves. . . . we find our bliss by following our own deepest intuitions, longings, and leadings.
—James W. Fowler[1]

Likewise the Spirit helps us in our weakness; for we do not know how to pray as we ought, but that very Spirit intercedes with sighs too deep for words.
—Romans 8:26

A calling commands that we attach ourselves to something bigger than ourselves, something that is infinite and lasting, so we can escape the life we thought we deserved and replace it with the life that we were meant for.

Richard Pimentel discovers this truth in childhood while thinking he is destined to be a hero. Instead of becoming a hero immediately, he becomes a brilliant public speaker who is driven to escape his troubled past. It is only when

The Q.U.E.S.T. for Vocation

he embraces his past and accepts his life's calling that he becomes an unexpected hero for the disabled.

At birth, Richard is pronounced dead in the delivery room, but in a miraculous turn of events, he survives the first of many challenges in his life. His mother, who is schizophrenic, has experienced three miscarriages before his birth. She leaves Richard in an orphanage, as she is unable to come to terms with his existence. Richard's father removes him from the orphanage and becomes his sole caretaker. After his father's death, Richard is raised by his impoverished grandmother and deemed "retarded" by a school guidance counselor. From these early traumatic experiences, Richard does not speak a word until he is six years old.

Pimentel soon realizes that he has a remarkable gift for public speaking. Pimentel's idol is College Bowl founder Ben Padrow, but upon trying out for Dr. Padrow, the ambitious young speaker is informed by his idol that he will not have anything to talk about until he has lived a full life.

Realizing that there is some merit to Dr. Padrow's observation, Pimentel subsequently enlists in the military and prepares for duty in Vietnam. Later, while fighting on the battlefield, Pimentel loses most of his hearing and is left with permanent tinnitus, a continual ringing in ears. He returns home frustrated. When others inform him that he will never achieve his dreams because of his loss of hearing, the determined veteran makes it his mission to prove them wrong.

But as Richard learns, his Q.U.E.S.T.$_{TM}$ is not as much about changing others' perceptions of persons with disabilities as it is about altering their perceptions of themselves, and with a little help from Art Honeyman, a fellow student, he receives his life's calling.

One night in 1972, Art, a foul-mouthed genius who is confined to a wheelchair due to cerebral palsy, phones Richard and tells him that it is his birthday and all he wants is pancakes. Richard agrees to take Art to what is supposedly the best pancake house in town. After Richard hauls Art up forty steps, they both head into the restaurant, only to be greeted by the disgusted stares of both the staff and the other patrons.

A waitress tells them that the establishment has the right to refuse service to anyone, and that they should leave. Richard argues for Art, saying,

> But we just want pancakes. We're not going to cause anyone trouble; we heard this was the best pancake house in town, and we want some pancakes. Our money is as good as anyone else's.

The waitress scoffs and heartlessly tells Art that he should have died at birth. She adds that if they do not leave *now*, she will call the police. With some effort, Art throws a quarter on the table and says, "Call them." Both Art and Richard are arrested under a law on the books at the time that basically made it illegal to be "ugly in public." As a result of this encounter, Richard redoubles his efforts to make workplaces more disabled-friendly. He gets a call from the President's Oval Office and begins working on the text that will become the Americans with Disabilities Act of 1990.

The poet Oliver Wendell Holmes once observed, "Most people go to their graves with their music still inside them." Because Richard's disabilities are permanent, Art encourages him not to overcome them, but rather to learn from them. The "music" that Richard finds enables him to begin a movement that culminates in the passing of the Americans with Disabilities Act. In listening to his "music," Richard helps improve the lives of disabled people across the country, as well as his own life. Richard shares his "music" rather than allowing it to follow him to his grave.

The Music Within

As we learn from *Music Within*[2], the 2007 film based on Richard Pimentel's life's story, finding the "music within" entails finding a way to share one's life's calling with the world. Much of this "music" centers on our soul's expression, how it is growing and changing us, how it points out what is most important to us. If we listen closely, we can find a way to share it.

Perhaps what Oliver Wendell Holmes was trying to tell us is that it takes a certain amount of courage to "sing out loud" when we are not sure how our music is going to be received. Will it be appreciated, or will it be laughed at? Will it be minimized, or discarded or shot down? Even if it is celebrated, that can be scary, too. Finding the music within is another way of talking about listening to the voice of vocation and calling, and this search requires us to "live an undivided life."

Living an Undivided Life

The traumatic experiences of a suicide mission during a rocket attack in Vietnam, which leave Richard deaf, combined with his being turned down for the GI Bill for college admissions because he has lost his hearing, throws Richard off-track. Somewhere in my own life, I had also been knocked off-track. In similar fashion to the detonation of a deadly gamma bomb, which split my favorite comic book character, the Hulk, into the undivided life of a raging monster and detached yet brilliant scientist, I had been assailed by years of unsuspected and undiagnosed high blood pressure that bombarded my kidneys with inflammation, causing them to weaken and eventually fail. This disease was the catalyst that set me on a Q.U.E.S.T.™

in search of a hidden wholeness of emotional health, meaning, and creativity.

As Richard discovers while searching for his "music," I, too, began the process of examining my life and discovered an absence that found me wanting in spiritual depth and power. This discovery forced me to take the courageous inward Q.U.E.S.T.$_{TM}$ to find and follow my bliss.

Follow Your Bliss

The phrase "follow your bliss" is one of Joseph Campbell's most identifiable and most quoted sayings. He sees this not merely as a mantra, but also as a helpful guide to the individual along the hero journey that each of us walks through life:

> If you follow your bliss, you put yourself on a kind of track that has been there all the while, waiting for you, and the life that you ought to be living is the one you are living. Wherever you are—if you are following your bliss, you are enjoying that refreshment, that life within you, all the time.

What Campbell means by "bliss" is that burning need that people are passionate about and seek to fulfill. It involves an intuitive, deep-down way of knowing what is right for us, what is good for us, what makes us "happy." He emphasizes what we ourselves know on that intuitive level—that we will not be truly happy, we will not have a sense of personal fulfillment, unless we *are* following our bliss, unless we are doing with our lives what we know we want to be doing, being how we know we want to be, living by the values we know are our ultimate values.

Campbell encourages his students to "follow their bliss" in matters of vocation. Though he has sometimes been criticized by people who do not understand what it might mean to do so, his advice is rooted in the conviction that feelings of joy, vitality, and passionate desire are some of the most important criteria for discerning whether or not we are on the path of our true calling.

Far from suggesting the irresponsibility of moving from one pleasure to another, "follow your bliss" is advice ideally leading to a life's commitment—as it did for Campbell when he followed his love of mythology. In considering whether a certain path is meant for us, we must consult our heart, asking ourselves, "Is my heart in this path?" and have the courage to listen to the music within that gives us the deepest sense of harmony.

Unfortunately, however, we all know the people who have stopped listening to their own music and bliss, and who listen only to others to learn what they ought to do, how to behave, and what values to live for. Like them, we, too, are tempted to sacrifice our own music and bliss for those of another. When we give in to this temptation—maybe because it is the easy road or because we feel obliged—we lose the connection and eventually forget the sound and the feel of its call. We no longer feel its urgings.

Questions
1. Richard Pimentel has several challenges, both physical and people's perceptions, to overcome. His efforts to overcome those ultimately lead him to discover the "music within." What obstacles have you had to overcome to discover your "music within"?

2. Art Honeywell unknowingly serves as a mentor to Richard to help him listen to the "music within." Have you unknowingly served as a mentor to someone else to help them to listen to the "music within"? If so, how were you able to listen to your own "music within" to assist someone else with the process?

3. What does Oliver Wendell Holmes's observation "Most people go to their graves with their music still inside them" mean to you?

Notes
1. James Fowler. Weaving the New Creation: Stages of Faith and the Public Church. (Eugene: Wipf and Stock Publishers, 1991).

2. Music Within. Dir. Steven Sawalich. Perf. Ron Livingston, Melissa George, and Michael Sheen. Lionsgate, 2007. Film.

Part Four

The Call to Meaningful Work

☙

CHAPTER FOURTEEN

The Journey to a Career and Calling

ಬಿ

Here's a chance to make it,
If we focus on our goals.
If you dish it, we can take it;
Just remember—you've been told.
It's a different world from where you come from.

—Bill Cosby, Stu Gardner, and Dawnn Lewis[1]

Then Amos answered Amaziah, "I am no prophet, nor a prophet's son; but I am a herdsman, and a dresser of sycamore trees, and the Lord took me from following the flock, and the Lord said to me, 'Go, prophesy to my people Israel.'"

—Amos 7:14-15

Every time that I attend a conference of some sort, I find myself introducing myself to a new person and telling what I do for a living. After shaking his or her hands and learning what the other person does for a living, I complete the ritual encounter by exchanging business cards. At first glance, this may not seem like a strange ritual of introduction. But on further investigation, I have always found it strange that the ritual of introducing ourselves to another quickly moves from a personal identity to a set of roles that we perform.

Vocation, as we have seen, is more about who we are than about what we happen to do. Our careers seldom are the same thing as our life's calling. For many (if not most) people, a career is the job we do in order to provide for our families, but it is not necessarily who we are or what we are called to be.

For instance, I am a United Methodist minister. I earn my living by providing a number of services to the college where I work and to several other local congregations as a consultant. Some of those services are closely related to my call, and some are not. I think that I have gifts for preaching, teaching, and writing. I also believe that I am a compassionate person and am reasonably effective as a leader. I often feel called to walk with people during the difficult times of their lives on their $Q.U.E.S.T._{TM}$ to find meaning and purpose. But being a minister is not, strictly speaking, my calling; it is my career. I believe that my primary calling in life is to be the artist that I was born to be. The problem was, especially in those early years of my life, I did not know what kind of artist I was supposed to become. All I knew was that drawing—especially

The Journey to a Career and Calling

superhero and cartoon characters—was sort of a calling to me in my pre-teen and adolescent years, and I was known throughout school as the student who could really draw.

When I entered the twelfth grade, my mother convinced me that "there was no money in art." After I heard this, my interest in becoming a professional artist waned, but I never forgot my initial desire to be an artist. Years later, as I got older, this "longing to be an artist" urge was never too far behind. In fact, when I enrolled in college, I did so as a frustrated artist who needed to find a new sense of purpose.

College is a Different World

College is a different world from what most high school students are accustomed to or are ready to experience. It is a place where a student enters her freshman year thinking that she has been called to be a doctor and thus begins pre-medical studies. It is only when she makes a "C" in her first biology course that her notion of being "called" to be a doctor changes and she begins the discernment process of trying to discover where her life is leading her.

In looking back over her college experience, Deborah, a senior in her fall semester, discusses her discernment process of finding meaningful work:

> If you had asked me where God was leading me four years ago, that would have been an easy answer. "Speech

pathology" was the direction that I believed I was going in. If you had asked me two years ago where God was leading me, I would have said into "Art Education," because I love art and I love children. If you ask me today where I think God is leading me, I will tell you that I just don't know.

As the struggle to "know where God is leading" Deborah indicates, regardless of a student's reason for being on campus, college serves as a transforming and turning point where students will wrestle with new ideas, discover new interests, and explore issues of identity and intimacy to make sense out of their lives. Erica, a senior education major, is twenty-two, and she reflects on her collegiate experience thus:

> College is a time [when] you experiment with life and discern what direction God has for you. No matter what people you meet, friends you lose, [or] experience you have, God will always be there for you.

Another student, Tamera, a freshman math major, concurs with the "experimental nature" of college life. She expresses this in her need to adjust to dorm life:

> College has been a big adjustment. I have been learning to live with new people who are constantly around. The people in the dorm don't just go away. I have never really and truly had to share my personal space like I do now. I believe that God has a plan for me and that

The Journey to a Career and Calling

everything happens for a reason, but right now I am not sure what dorm life has to do with that.

Similar to the experience that these three students describe, my college experience was also a call to adventure and to a different world than I had been accustomed to. It felt a lot like being lost in space, and I needed a guidance system to help me to navigate through the unfamiliarity of college life. And like most concerned parents of a college student, my mother was only too happy to assist me in any way that she could.

For her, this meant constantly providing me with information that she believed would help me when I was out on my own. Following this impulse, when it was time for me to go off to college, my mother encouraged me to pursue a degree that would enable me to get a job upon graduation. Eager to please my mother and having a love for video games, I decided to go into the field of electronic engineering. My rationale for this odd decision was thus:

- *The graphics in the video games were similar to the comic books and cartoons that I loved;*
- *Most, if it not all, of the video games involved electronic and computer technology; and*
- *The computer industry was growing, and I was convinced that majoring in this field would help me to get a job after graduation.*

The Q.U.E.S.T. for Vocation

Just when I thought that I had everything figured out, I had two experiences during my freshman year that changed the direction of my life.

The first experience happened during my first psychology class for the general education requirement when I became fascinated with human behavior. The notion of the "unconscious processes" that influence human behavior was something that resonated with me at a gut level. In fact, when I would go to the library to study after class, I found that daydreaming and observing interactions going on around me were much more interesting than doing calculus or any other assignment for the day.

Call it being nosy or being extremely interested in what makes people tick, but I was hooked on this strange new interest. The next semester, when I took "Western Civilization and Culture," the same thing occurred. Instead of reading electronic schematics, scientific proofs, and mathematical theorems, I became more interested in learning about people, their patterns of behavior, customs, rituals, and stories. Over the next few months of enduring other core curriculum classes, the "distraction" of human behavior continued to interfere with my career goal of becoming an engineer.

In addition to my class experiences, an unlikely off-campus encounter provided yet another distraction. While I was playing a favorite video game at the mall arcade, two girls approached me with a religious pamphlet entitled *How to Know God*. Not wanting to lose my game, I tossed the pamphlet to the side, briefly spoke to the girls, and continued to play.

After the game was over, I picked up the pamphlet and quickly decided to find the girls to return the pamphlet, as I thought that they had given it to the wrong person. I searched the mall over but was unsuccessful in locating the girls. I sat in the food court of the mall, trying to make sense of my encounter, when I was suddenly overcome with emotion that I could not explain. I had a hunch that something or someone was calling me. But what was I being called to do? More importantly, how was I to be sure of what or who was calling?

Like most college students, I had no idea about what my calling was or what I wanted out of life. I was simply following my mother's wishes without really thinking about what it meant or whether or not it was right for me. To make matters worse, I was still struggling to make sense of my video arcade experience, which seemed to be knocking me even further "off- track" from the course that my mother had prescribed.

Little did I know that these "off-track" experiences would reawaken my forgotten artistic desire that had kept me so engaged during my childhood, when using my imagination had led to a talent of being creative.

This desire, which seemed in opposition to electronic engineering, would ultimately lay the groundwork of my philosophy for life. In a strange way, these "off-track" experiences seemed to be inviting me to combine the best of electronic engineering, filled with logic, reason, objectivity, and critical thinking and my childhood artistic desire for creativity, imagination, connecting patterns, and trusting my hunches.

As with my experience, thousands of college students have also encountered being knocked "off-track" from following a predetermined path, only to discover something important about themselves. On average, college students change their majors two or more times during their college years before deciding what they want to do.

The good news is that in the midst of changing majors, through trial and error and different experiences inside and outside the classroom, students will begin to fashion and live out some type of philosophy for life. Often this philosophy will emerge from a mixture of ideas from parents, other authority figures, and gut feelings.

It is often through questions such as "What do you want to be when you grow up?" that students begin to think about their lives in terms of an occupation. And of course, when asking these questions, people do not really mean "What do you want to *be*," but rather they mean, "What do you want to *do* for a living?" This is another way of asking

The Journey to a Career and Calling

"What career do you want to pursue?", which is often confused with "What do you want to do with your life?" On the surface these two questions seem very similar, but underneath the surface the difference between a *career* and a *calling* can be found.

Finding a Calling out of a Career

The words *career* and *calling* are often used interchangeably. However, a closer look at the definition of the words provides some clarity. For instance, the word *career* comes from the Latin word for "cart" and the Middle French word for "racetrack," which implies "running or moving at full speed." In other words, a person can "career" around a track for a long time but never get anywhere. A career is a "track" or a line of work and addresses the question "What do you want to do for a living?" A person can—and many times does—have different careers at different points in life.

Answering a *calling* is completely different from identifying a career or an occupation. While a *career* has more to do with earning money and paying the rent, a *calling* is tied to our sense of meaning and life purpose. A calling addresses the questions "What do you want to be?" and "What do you want to do with your life?"

For most of us, a calling is synonymous with being called by God, who speaks to our hearts in a compelling way, beckoning us to *listen* and *follow*. In his book *Wishful Thinking: A Seeker's ABC*[2], Presbyterian minister and writer Frederick Buechner puts it this way: "The place God calls you is the place where your deep gladness and the world's deep hunger meet." This "deep gladness" is at the heart of the matter and is often explained as either as the passion we might have for a particular subject or issue, or the joy we find when using our innate gifts and talents.

Parker Palmer expands on Buechner's notion of vocation in his book *Let Your Life Speak*[3]; he suggests that the discovery of vocation or a life's calling comes from listening to our life telling us who we are and what we are meant to do. Rather than an external voice calling us to who we are meant to be, Palmer focuses on listening and reflecting upon a person's true self, including personality characteristics, gifts, skills, aptitudes, desires, passions, and interests.

Looking back on my college days, I learned the difference between a career and a calling, and recognized that the two words did not have to be at odds with each other. My mother's desire that I earn a credential to get myself employment after graduation was an important driving force that led to a career. Upon graduation, I was employed with a computer company that regularly asked me to stretch the truth in order to maximize profits.

For several months, I was pulled in two different directions: my sense of morality on one end, and my need to have a job on the other. But in the end, the decision was made for me, as I was laid off. Losing my job was a major factor in helping me to discern what I came to understand as my life's calling that first began with my artistic love of comic books and epic stories and culminated in the encounter with the two girls in the video arcade room.

It turned out that being an electronic engineer was not my life's calling. Instead, my love for comic books, my courses in psychology and cultural studies, my emerging religious faith, and my desire to help people make sense of life all came together to convince me to pursue a call to use my imagination as an ordained minister to help people make sense of life.

I had finally figured out what kind of artist I was to become: one who uses the imagination to help transform the human canvas of the soul. My engineering degree had provided me with a career, but now it was opening doors for me to fulfill my calling in a new career as a minister.[4] I had come full circle and discovered the truth of author Paula D'Arcy's statement that *"God comes to you disguised as your life."*

Embracing a life's calling is a lifelong process. It takes patience and courage to pay attention to the experiences and stories that are constantly emerging from the text of our lives—especially if the stories and experiences run contrary to a predetermined path. There will be times when

The Q.U.E.S.T. for Vocation

we see only partial glimpses and not the entire picture. Be careful not to be thrown "off-track" by all of the noises and distractions that may be part of your dream and your ambition. Our life's calling is to use our passions, gifts, and talents to meet a need in the world.

Questions
1. Have there been some "off-track" experiences in your life? Is there any way that you could reframe those experiences and begin to see them as critical learning experiences to help discern a life's calling?

2. Being an electronic engineer was not my life's calling. Recall times when you discovered that you were not living your life's calling. What was helpful to you as you worked your way through these situations?

3. There are times during discerning a life's calling when doors are closed to us. Is there a closed door in your life right now? How are you dealing with it? Is it possible that God may be using this disappointment to offer you something new and unexpected?

Notes
1. Bill Cosby, Stu Gardner, and Dawnn Lewis. "A Different World." Theme song from A Different World, Carsey-Werner Productions. September 1987-July 1993.

2. Frederick Buechner. Wishful Thinking: A Seeker's ABC. (San Francisco: HarperOne, 1993).

3. Parker Palmer. Let Your Life Speak: Listening to Voice of Vocation. (San Francisco: JosseyBass, 2000).

4. In the United Methodist tradition, ordained ministers must have a college degree and attend seminary to obtain a master of divinity degree. Attending DeVry provided me with the stepping stone that I needed to be accepted into Candler School of Theology at Emory University.

Chapter Fifteen

The Call to Serve the Church

In the evening I went very unwillingly to a society in Aldersgate Street, where one was reading Luther's preface to the Epistle to the Romans. About a quarter before nine, while he was describing the change which God works in the heart through faith in Christ, I felt my heart strangely warmed. I felt I did trust in Christ, Christ alone, for salvation; and an assurance was given me that He had taken away my sins, even mine, and saved me from the law of sin and death.

—John Wesley[1]

As [Jesus] walked by the Sea of Galilee, he saw two brothers, Simon, who is called Peter, and Andrew his brother, casting a net into the sea—for they were fishermen. And he said to them, "Follow me, and I will make you fish for people." Immediately they left their nets and followed him. As he went from there, he saw two other brothers, James, son of Zebedee, and his brother, John, in the boat with their father, Zebedee, mending their nets, and he called them. Immediately they left the boat and their father, and followed him.

—Matthew 4: 18-22

The Call to Serve the Church

Growing up in the Black church, I assumed that there were two calls: the call to be a disciple of Jesus, and the call to be a preacher. I answered the call to follow Jesus, the "smeared one"[2] (the seldom used translated word from the titles "Christ" and "Messiah") by pledging my allegiance to Him as Lord and Savior, like several of my church friends during Confirmation class. But I did not want anything to do with the second call: the call to be a preacher! No one told me that answering the call to follow Jesus would constantly challenge my assumptions, requiring me to keep my ego in check.

I learned that a theological approach to a life's calling involves ideas of the transcendent, of purpose, and of community. To receive a call means someone outside myself is calling; what I am to do in response to that call provides me with purpose; and this call and response occur within and are guided by my larger community. In the fullest sense of the word, a vocation includes my occupation (whether in church or in parish ministry, or as a gardener or as a physician), but it also involves my civic responsibilities, family life, church participation, leisure practices, and consumer habits.

My encounter with the girls in the arcade room that I discussed in the previous chapter and other encounters seemed to converge together, and I believed that God was calling me to be an ordained minister. I went to seminary to develop the skills to fulfill this call. One slight problem occurred when I came to the end of my seminary education: I did not have a church appointment, and no one was calling me for potential interviews.

The majority of my classmates all had appointments waiting for them upon graduation. Without an appointment to serve either as the minister in charge or as an associate minister, I could not fulfill my call because I would not be able to be ordained by the denomination.

I prayed to God for an appointment, and I went on several interviews for associate minister positions. I was turned down from all of them. Then the call came. The senior minister from the Gainesville First United Methodist Church in Gainesville, Georgia, a predominately white church in my hometown, wanted to interview me for an associate position that the church was creating.

Being a native of Gainesville, I was familiar with the church, as they had a working relationship with my home church, and we had joint confirmation classes and youth service projects together. I felt as if the Gainesville church was doing ministry in a way that went beyond race, class, and social standing, and I wanted to be part of it. I went to the interview and met with several key members of the church. I walked away from the interview feeling that I had been called to be the associate of the church. I was offered the position and was ordained all in a matter of weeks.

The Call to Serve the Church

Being the First

I was the first minister of outreach and missions that the Gainesville church had ever hired. Strangely, my being the first person in this position was not the buzz around the city. Rather, it was that I was the first Black person that the church had ever hired as a minister. For the first time, I was forced to see how my calling, which included my personal experiences as a Black person, would either connect or disconnect me from the church and from larger society.

I still have the framed article from the local newspaper, *The Times*, hanging in my office, announcing my appointment to the Gainesville First United Methodist Church. The headline from the "Religion Today" section reads: **"Man's Ordination is a Milestone: Church to have its first black associate pastor."**[3] The reporter began the article saying, "God knows no color, and members of the United Methodist Church are reflecting that through their cross-racial appointments." When the appointment was made, Charles Wilson, the District Superintendent of the Gainesville District, was quoted as saying, "The significance of this [appointment] is to get what we call 'cross-racial appointments' to improve race relations and cultural understanding."

I was not as concerned as the media and the community were about my being the first Black minister at the church. I simply saw this as a great opportunity for me to learn

The Q.U.E.S.T. for Vocation

about ministry. Working under an experienced minister, I would have the opportunity to learn about the interworking of a large church staff and congregation.

I really did not have a lot of difficulty while serving at Gainesville. As I reflect back on my experiences, part of the reason may have been that Gainesville was my hometown and several of the members of the church knew my father, a local businessman in the community. Another reason may have been that the church's leadership was progressive in its outlook on ministry and the world. But perhaps the most compelling reason for my success may have been that I was equipped with the transferable skills of communicating effectively, a keen understanding of human nature, and the ability to analyze a problem and think outside the box to find creative solutions. All of these skills were required to help me adapt to the congregation.

The Feelings of Twoness

Two years later, I was called by the bishop and told that I was moving. The bishop appointed me to LaGrange College, a United Methodist Church-related school that is the oldest private college in Georgia, as its first full-time chaplain. I was surprised by this move, as I had always felt that God called me to be a preacher in a local church. But now, the calling to serve the church seemed to be in jeopardy, as the bishop moved me away from the church and onto a college campus.

Shortly after the bishop's move was made official, the *LaGrange Daily News*, the local newspaper, published an article announcing my arrival to LaGrange College, stating:

> "Rev. Brown has a strong desire to incorporate a 'hands-on' approach to the needs of individuals and has a unique ability to diagnose the needs of others," President Stuart Gulley said. "He is highly qualified and capable to expand and enhance the religious life of LaGrange College."[4]

Aside from being the first full-time chaplain in this position, I was also the first and only Black male in the senior level administration. Although I did not think much about this when I arrived, it did not take long for me to realize the potential for difficulty that I could face as young adult under thirty years of age coming into a newly created administrative position. It was also a struggle as I recognized the gap in the social standing and economic opportunities between the Whites and Blacks in the community. Since the College employed me, I found myself in an economic situation much different from that of the majority of Blacks in the community. Later, I would be

A Disturbing Church Experience

On Sunday mornings I preached at the blended worship service at the First United Methodist Church in LaGrange and then would preach at the chapel for the students at the college. When I was not preaching at the church or the college chapel, I would fill in as a visiting preacher for churches in the LaGrange area.

One Sunday, within six months of arriving at the College, I preached at one of the nearby Black churches. After the sermon, I was approached by an elderly woman. She greeted me warmly and told me that she and the rest of the church were so proud of me and happy that I was at the College. She went on to talk about my appointment to the College as being a historical event, since I was the first Black person in that position.

As soon as she finished her complimentary statement, however, the next words that she spoke knocked me off of my feet. She asked, "Have the folks at the College given you the ['N-word'] test yet?" Knowing nothing of any test, I responded, "I don't think I understand what you are talking about." She replied, "You know, the test when 'they' give you authority and power, and then suddenly take it away from you when you try to use it, leaving

The Call to Serve the Church

you as powerless as a 'token.'" She walked away. I stood bewildered, unable to move.

This experience really got under my skin. I wondered whether or not I had done the right thing by answering the call to come to LaGrange, only to face such oppositional thinking from my own people. Since my encounter with the Klan in high school, I had been mentally and emotionally prepared to confront racism. But nothing in my background had prepared me to confront this type of thinking from my own people. As I tried to understand the elderly lady's perspective, which was no doubt based on her experience, I began to understand what sociologist and historian W.E.B. DuBois meant in *The Souls of Black Folks* when he wrote:

> One ever feels his twoness—an American, a Negro; two souls, two thoughts, two unreconciled strivings; two warring ideals in one dark body, whose dogged strength alone keeps it from being torn asunder.[5]

Adjusting to this new setting was challenging. I spent several years examining my call to the College and my assumptions about what it meant to be a college chaplain. It was a struggle to be comfortable in my own skin in all situations.

Much of what I was struggling with was my own need to fit in and integrate my formative experiences so that I could discern my calling at the College. I came to understand that my calling included finding my own identity and how it related to race, as well as an emerging theology of justice balanced with tolerance, grace, compassion, and forgiveness. Meanwhile, as I was working to discern my identity that was changing, the members of the College community were also going through a change and had to adjust to what it meant to have a full-time chaplain.

The Examined Life

After I began working on this college campus, it was not very long before I was called to learn classical Greek and Western philosophical thought. If I was going to be a successful college chaplain and assist students in developing a faith that sought understanding and meaning through using scripture, critical thinking, church tradition and personal experience, then I had to come to terms with the strong influence of Greek philosophy on the academy.

In those early years, I had no idea what it meant to be a college chaplain or how the nuances of the academic world, influenced by Greek philosophy to focus on critical thinking, could work alongside faith. My job description was not any help to me with this puzzle. It simply said: "To tend to the spiritual needs of the campus." After receiving this mandate from the president and the trustees, I was

The Call to Serve the Church

embarrassed that I still did not know what it meant to be a college chaplain.

During my first week on the job, I began to read everything that I could about the subject. My search did not provide any information, since there was not a great deal of published material on what it meant to be a college chaplain.

In desperation, I did an Internet search on the word *chaplain* and found a story about a compassionate fourth-century holy man named Martin, who grew up as a "military brat." His father was in the Roman imperial army, and so from a young age Martin was exposed to the military lifestyle.

While serving in the Roman army, Martin had an experience that started him on a Q.U.E.S.T.™. Once, while riding on his horse through what is now modern-day France, he encountered a beggar. The only clothes Martin had were those he was wearing, so he took his cloak (the Latin word for "cloak" is where we get the words *chapel* and *chaplain*) and cut it in half for the beggar. That night, Martin dreamed of Jesus wearing the half-cloak he had given to the beggar, and when he awoke, his cloak was fully restored. From these experiences, Martin determined that his faith prohibited him from fighting, and he answered his life's calling of being a priest.

After reading this, I intuitively connected the dots of my own story of wanting to help others and being a creative

The Q.U.E.S.T. for Vocation

thinker to the story of St. Martin showing compassion to others. I decided that a chaplain had something to do with imagination and following God's nudges to prompt us to share parts of ourselves to meet the spiritual, physical, intellectual, and emotional needs of others. So I followed my hunch and decided to play at my job, saying to myself, "Well, since I do not know what it means to be a college chaplain, and no one else seems to have written anything about it, then I might as well have fun trying to figure it out."[6]

Inspiring the Soul

My way of "figuring out" how to meet the spiritual needs of the campus involved a leap of faith and the trial and error process of using my imagination. This involved listening to the voices of a lot of people and risking being misunderstood by thinking outside the box, such as turning the traditional 11:00 a.m. chapel service on its head by beginning a student-led praise and worship service on Sundays at 10:00 p.m.

The idea for the service occurred when the attendance at the traditional 11:00 a.m. chapel service dwindled down to two people: my wife and me. By providing an 11:00 a.m. service, I was following a mandate that was given to me by the president. Within five months of this mandate, however, I realized that things had to change, but I did not yet know what that meant or what a new service would look like.

One Sunday around 9:30 p.m., I went back to the college to pick up a book that I had left in my office. While driving to the campus, I noticed that everything in town was closed. Arriving on the campus, I was surprised to see several students huddled around a small building near the edge of campus. Curious about the crowd, I went to find out what was going on and discovered students doing laundry.

I recalled from my college days that I did laundry only when I absolutely had to. I thought that if these students were anything like me and my friends during college, they would gladly find any way of getting out of laundry duty! And that is when it occurred to me: we will have chapel on Sundays at 10:00 p.m.! I figured that 10:00 p.m. would be a perfect time to have a chapel service. Since the fraternity houses were closed on Sundays, and the last movie at the local theater was over by 9:30 p.m. on Sundays, there would be nothing to compete for the students' interest to prohibit them from attending the chapel service.

Even though I was questioned by several college administrators for not having a traditional 11:00 a.m. worship service for students, I was pursuing a holy hunch by acting on what I believed to be God's nudge. In doing so, I had to suspend my rational self and took the chance of appearing foolish by offering a worship service that was entirely student-oriented at a time that was convenient for their schedules.

Much like Jesus' disciples, who followed a hunch and abandoned their fishing occupations for the uncertain promises of a wandering prophet, I, too, acted on a holy hunch by creating a chapel service to meet the campus's spiritual needs. Over time, I became quite good at "tending to the spiritual needs," or so I thought.

When I received my three-year evaluation from several members of the college community, including faculty, staff, students, alumni, and administration, I was astounded by their assessment of me and my work. I received a very negative evaluation and felt as if I were being personally attacked from comments such as "He depends too much on talent. He lacks leadership skills. And we don't know what he does as chaplain."

Challenging the Mind

I discovered that the college valued a different set of assumptions, assumptions that focused on philosophy, scholarship, research, and analytical thinking that was counter to the listening for life's calling, trusting holy hunches, and acting on divine nudges that I was accustomed to doing. Chief among this academic philosophy was the Socratic method, a form of inquiry and debate between

The Call to Serve the Church

individuals with opposing viewpoints based on asking and answering questions to stimulate critical thinking and to illuminate ideas. It searches for general, commonly held truths that shape opinion and scrutinizes them to determine their consistency with other beliefs. The basic form is a series of questions formulated as tests of logic and fact, intended to help a person or group discover their beliefs about some topic.

As a philosopher, Socrates was famous for saying that "the unexamined life, a life that avoids the questions, is not worth living." He said this at his trial for heresy, when he was accused of having encouraged his students to challenge the accepted beliefs of the time and to think for themselves. The sentence was death, but Socrates had the option of suggesting an alternative punishment. He could have chosen life in prison or exile and thus would likely have avoided death.

Socrates believed that these alternatives would rob him of the only thing that made life useful: examining the world around him and discussing how to make the world a better place. Without his "examined life," there was no point in living. So he suggested that Athens reward him for his service to society. The result, of course, is that they voted for a punishment of death instead.

Similar to my understanding of St. Martin's story, which influenced my view of how to be a college chaplain,

I applied the same process to understand Socrates' life story and calling. I determined that he believed that the purpose of human life was personal and spiritual growth. Armed with the comments from my evaluation and the insight into Socrates' life, I was able to create a new philosophy that combined academic scholarship and living faith together. This involved a balance of my head and heart that was responsive to trusting my natural inclination to follow holy hunches and to listen for God's calling as well as the academy's interest in research and analysis, critical thinking, and searching for commonly held truths.

Live the Questions

Ever since I was eight years old, my mother insisted that I "pay attention, watch people, and ask questions." Partially due to my introspective and imaginative nature, my mother planted seeds that encouraged me to seek understanding and not to be afraid to ask questions. German poet Rainer Rilke talks about examining life's experiences by asking questions in his book *Letters to a Young Poet*.

The book consisted of ten letters written to Franz Kappus, a nineteen-year-old officer cadet trying to choose between a literary career and entering the Austro-Hungarian Army at the Vienna Military Academy, of which Rilke was an alumnus. Discouraged by the prospect of life in the Austro-Hungarian Army, Kappus began to send his poetry to the twenty-seven-year-old Rilke, seeking both literary criticism and career advice. In one of the most instructive responses to Kappus, Rilke exclaims:

> I beg you to have patience with everything unresolved in your heart and to try to love the questions themselves as if they were locked rooms or books written in a very foreign language. Don't search for the answers, which could not be given to you now, because you would not be able to live them. And the point is to live everything. Live the questions now. Perhaps then, someday far in the future, you will gradually, without even noticing it, live your way into the answer.[7]

Knowing nothing about Socrates or Rilke, my mother was instructive in providing a foundation for me to learn to think for myself by living the questions. My mother planted seeds that encouraged me to seek understanding and not to be afraid to ask questions.

By adding logic, reason, objectivity, and critical thinking to my desire to listen for God to give me a hunch, I continued to tend to the spiritual needs of the campus by "living the questions" of life. Exposure to the academic process of exploring questions helped me to notice connections between seemingly unconnected ideas of the faith and the academy. I had an "ah-ha" moment and understood Rilke's advice to Franz and "gradually, without even noticing it, live[d my] way into the answer."

The Q.U.E.S.T. for Vocation

Now, sixteen years later, I enjoy a good relationship with members of the College and the larger LaGrange community. My doubts have all been removed. I *had* done the right thing in answering the call to come to LaGrange College as its chaplain and now as its Vice President for Spiritual Life and Church Relations. In 2003, I received the national Chaplain of the Year Award, an annual award given by the United Methodist Higher Education Foundation to recognize innovative contributions to college chaplaincy and outstanding service in the 125 United Methodist-related colleges and universities across the country.

Answering my life's calling began with my imagination as a child and then developed into a love for comic books. My college experiences of classes and "off-track" experiences (which seemed to call me away from being an electronic engineer), together with my calling to ministry, where I struggled to be comfortable in my own skin, have helped me to complete the several quests that have transformed my life.

My Q.U.E.S.T.$_{TM}$ to serve the church forced me to look at life through the lenses of faith and trust by listening to God's nudges, holy hunches, and a series of callings to discern a personal *vocation*. Discerning the meaning behind kidney disease (which necessitated the need for dialysis and two kidney transplants), accepting my acceptance from God (which includes being a right-brained person who loves superheroes), and undergoing my difficult experiences of society and culture have helped to shape my identity.

The questions of identity, purpose, and meaning that stirred me at different points on my Q.U.E.S.T.$_{TM}$ for vocation have all been transformed into the answer of my life's calling: using the imagination to connect with the metaphorical and symbolic world of images, universal human patterns of stories, and feelings to help others on their Q.U.E.S.T.$_{TM}$ And in perpetual response to the call to "face the sun" that came to me so many years ago, I continue to help others to listen for *The Voice* that calls each of us to be at one with God, ourselves, and the world.

Questions
1. What comes to mind when you think of formative influences in your life? Are there any particular values or attitudes you learned from your family, your culture, or your religious upbringing that you still hold on to?

2. My early experiences with racism helped to shape my identity. What life experiences have taught you most about who you are and what you have to offer? What more do you need to learn about yourself? How might you go about learning it? Who might be able to help you?

3. Describe in a sentence what you believe your calling in life really is. How much of your calling can you currently pursue in your job or career? If you are an

older adult, is there a call that you have not pursued before that you can now consider?

Notes
1. John Wesley. Editor Percy Livingstone Parker, "I Felt My Heart Strangely Warmed," Journal of John Wesley. (Chicago: Moody Press, 1951).

2. The word Christ is the title given to Jesus of Nazareth. It is the anglicized form of the Greek word Christos, which is the translation of the Hebrew/Aramaic word Messiah. To say that Jesus is the Christ (Greek) is the same as saying that Jesus is the Messiah (Hebrew). But what does Christ/Messiah mean in plain English? When the term is translated (rather than transliterated), we have a common English word that corresponds to Christ and Messiah, as the one who is "smeared" or "anointed." Like all our religious words, smeared and anointed were ordinary secular words before they were adopted for religious purposes and filled with religious meaning. It may sound peculiar or even irreverent, but to say in English that "Jesus is the Christ" or "Jesus is the Messiah" is the same as saying "Jesus is the smeared one" or "Jesus is the anointed one." M. Eugene Boring, Disciples and the Bible: A History of Disciples Biblical Interpretation in North America. (St. Louis: Chalice Press 1997).

3. The Times, "Religion Today" section, Friday, June 9, 1995. Lolita Browning.

4. LaGrange Daily News, Saturday, May 10, 1997.

5. W.E.B. Du Bois. The Souls of Black Folks, (Chicago: A.C. McClurg & Company, 1903).

6. When I was "playing" at meeting the spiritual needs of the campus, I was more curious and open-minded without having a pre-described or pre-determined outcome in mind. I was trusting God to provide.

7. Rainer Maria Rilke. Letters to a Young Poet, trans. M.D. Herter. (New York: Norton, 1993).

Conclusion

☙

Over the course of the preceding chapters, we have come to see that vocation or a life's calling is not a detailed blueprint imposed on our lives from above. Neither is it a hidden plan, neatly stored away in the attic waiting for a special season for us to stumble upon it by accident while looking for something else. Rather, our vocation is in front of us. It *is* me—my life lived in harmony with God's gifts, my talents, passions, abilities, and perceived needs of the world.

Some Christian traditions suggest that vocation is about getting people saved. The main question that is asked from this perspective, or so it seems, has to do with your eternal destination. This is an important focus, but it is not the only emphasis to answering God's call. It has always seemed to me that my faith tradition is known for this perspective in addition to something more immediate. My faith tradition, the one in which I was raised, has always seemed to pay equal attention to what happens *after* a person is saved.

What is supposed to happen after we are saved is that we begin to live differently, gratefully, with a brand-new sense of meaning and purpose. And this is when we are following our vocation in life—the purpose that God saved us for.

In these chapters, I have described *vocation* in some very personal ways, though the truth is that vocation is never entirely personal. Sure, there are times where the discernment process of listening to our life's calling is extremely personal. But the focus is never entirely self-centered. Vocation is more than a personal endeavor, since ultimately it involves something bigger than ourselves: a focus that is directed outward towards God and neighbor.

Throughout my life, I have attempted to answer a life's calling that has taken me down different roads—ones that I never thought that I would travel. Along the way, I have had to reexamine what my life was trying to do with me. What about you? What have you been called to do with *your* life? To live our lives as a response to God's call is a pilgrimage, a shared journey with others that becomes a Q.U.E.S.T.$_{TM}$ for vocation. Thank you for taking this journey with me. I pray that your Q.U.E.S.T.$_{TM}$ for vocation takes you where God is calling you.